SHE HIT ___
WITH "WATCH ME ___ NOW ___
LORRIE MORGAN AND . . .

• GEORGE JONES . . . Lorrie took Tammy Wynette's place onstage with George just as his career was riding high, and his personal life was sinking fast. Now discover Lorrie's fear as fans rioted when he didn't show up for performances and her first look at how alcohol can destroy a man.

• MCA RECORDS . . . They wanted her to disown the Opry, Minnie Pearl and Bill Anderson. When she stood by her roots, they labeled her a bitch. Find out how her reputation suffered, and how she showed them that genuine gold turns platinum in the end . . .

• KEITH WHITLEY . . . Few couples in Nashville seemed more in love than Lorrie and Keith. Their friends hoped that Lorrie could save Keith from himself. See the heartbreaking truth of Lorrie's desperate efforts—even tying him to her as they slept—to stop Keith from drinking himself to death . . .

• DOLLY PARTON . . . The superstar tracked Lorrie down to sing a duet, and "We Both Walk"—a haunting, lyrical ride into a woman's life—started off a friendship that let both women shine.

• THE OTHER MEN SHE LOVED . . . A bus driver and a pro football player took a piece of her heart. But will she find happiness with her new man, a singer with amazing vocal talent and a huge capacity for love?

LORRIE MORGAN

ACE COLLINS

St. Martin's Paperbacks

LORRIE MORGAN

Copyright © 1998 by Ace Collins.

Cover photograph copyright © Ron Wolfson/London Features.

ISBN: 0-312-96608-3

Printed in the United States of America

St. Martin's Paperbacks edition/June 1998

10 9 8 7 6 5 4 3 2 1

*To Leigh Anne, who always
got me a ticket to the "circus."*

Chapter 1

Loretta Lynn Morgan was born either on June 27, 1959, or on the same month and day one year later in 1960. The mere fact that the year is now in debate points out the current state of country music, a field where Ms. Morgan has gained superstar status. In the long history of country music, every year has always made a difference. In the past, those years would have been measured in how long you had been in the business, how hard you had worked, how many one-nighters you had played, how you had *grown* with your recording career, and how many dues you had paid along the tour route. Age meant little and loyalty was a part of every facet of the business. The fans stayed with you, and so did the bookers and the record companies.

The country music of the past—and Lorrie Morgan was very familiar with country music's past—was a forgiving and nurturing business. A rookie might go years without making much noise on the charts and still find that his record label was looking out for just the right song that would make him a star. If you had potential and were willing to work, Music City stood by you. This was proven time and time again. It had taken more than five years to make Patsy Cline a star, and Mel Tillis had slaved for more than twice that long. Yet Music City waited on them, and several dozen others. Many of those, such as Kitty Wells, who had gotten second, third, fourth, and fifth chances, were now in the Hall of Fame.

Stardom meant something special in "Old Nashville" too. Once you did earn your place in the middle of the spotlight, you were assured a living for as long as you wanted to work. Fans would join your fan club and come out to your shows every time you were in the area. Disc jockeys got to know you personally and programmed your new songs when each new release came out. And the Opry gave you a homecoming each week. Age and experience were revered and youth was not worshipped. It was rarely ''what have you done for me lately,'' it was usually ''what have you done over the long haul.''

So while the dollars weren't as large, a star's place was assured. The hard work and effort, the hours spent getting to know fans on a personal basis, paid off with security. In the country music of the forties, fifties, and sixties, the men and women who generated yesterday's hits always had a place on the marquee and in the heart. But country music became big business and with the money came a complete disregard for Nashville's time-honored value system.

Now country music has grown out of the long-held ''honor your elders'' tradition. Old is out, experience is not that important, veterans are now anyone who had been in the business for a couple of years, and when a female star hits forty, she is generally thought of as a ''has been.'' In the big-dollar industry that is today's country music, there is a generation gap where most fans ignore the old hit makers and most radio stations won't play them. Like a used-up professional baseball player, yesterday's superstars are written off and released as soon as they quit making hits. A few of them have found some degree of acceptance in places like Branson, but none of them could spin the right combination to reclaim a recording career for a major label. And few of the ''new'' fans of country music even cared who they were and what they had done in the past.

Barbara Mandrell, if she had been a part of the previous generation of country music stars—those who came up with the likes of Marty Robbins and Loretta Lynn—once could have toured to packed houses on her name and long list of hits alone. She could have also continued to release records forever on a label that would have been grateful for her earlier success. Then she got caught in the country music generation trap. She was singing better than ever, her stage shows were electric, and she was still beautiful, yet in 1996 she was but a distant memory to a new generation of country music fans who cared nothing about dues, they simply wanted to latch on to the latest fad. Loyalty was no longer a part of the business and tenure meant nothing. If you were "old," you were put out to pasture.

As this trend grew and more and more people realized what was happening to the veteran stars, a number of artists' bios began to reflect the fear of growing old. Many began to shave a year or more off their birth dates (one male act actually erased nine years). This changing of the birth year wasn't strictly a matter of vanity, it was more often than not due to the realization that when a star approached forty they were being written off in the search for some other act that was younger and more hip. So, while all of her father's bios list Lorrie having been born in 1959, it was hardly surprising that Lorrie's latest issued press releases moved her birth to 1960. After all, in the competitive world of country music in the nineties, one needed to be as young as possible in order to insure a chance at a "long" career. And you had to get that needed time any way you could.

Lorrie was more aware than anyone of what had been lost when country music "grew up" and threw away most of its traditions. After all, Lorrie's dad had been a star long before the birth of his fifth and last child, an eight pound and three ounce little girl. So Lorrie had always known the business. She had known it when it was small, tight-knit, and friendly, and she had seen it grow into a monster that showed little compassion. She was in reality a child of country music. And to fully understand what made Lorrie the big star she is today, one had to know something about the family tradition that began more than five decades ago. This was the tradition that nurtured a star.

Lorrie's father, George Morgan, was born in Waverly, Tennessee, on June 28, 1924. Like a host of other southern families, the Morgans were caught in hard times during the Depression. In order for his father to find work in a factory that offered a steady wage, George's family left the south for Ohio in the mid-thirties. As they moved, they took more than just their furniture and clothes, they took their values and traditions too. Even in the north, where southern music was called "hillbilly" and people who sang that music were often referred to as "stupid hicks," the Morgan home was filled with the sounds of country music.

In spite of the fact that George was living in the Mid-west and most of the kids were jiving to the beat of the big bands, country music was practically the only music young George ever heard. As a teen, young Morgan killed many hours playing guitar and listening to music piped out from WSM in Nashville. To the boy the Opry must have seemed like a church and the performers had to have been heroes. He memorized the lyrics and learned the licks on an old guitar. Whenever he got the chance, he would share what he had memorized with his family and friends. Yet by and large, when George hit his teens, most of his friends made fun of his love of hillbilly music. As they listened to him strum an old guitar and sing, they told him that he was doing little more than wasting his time. They quickly found out that they were wrong! They had been wasting their time making fun of old George. He actually had been investing his hours in something that would make him famous.

In his mid-teens, George had played for so many local fairs, talent shows and showcases that he gained a reputation as a darn good singer. And long before any of his friends had even figured out what they were going to do after high school, the transplanted southern boy's music and local fame had grown to such a point that WAKR, an Akron radio station, had given young Morgan his own show. After a short but dynamically successful run at WAKR, George left for a better-paying gig up the road in Wooster. He was a local star and thousands tuned in daily to hear his smooth hillbilly sounds. Yet, if not for an infatuation with a teeny bopper, Morgan might never have become anymore than a regional radio host.

In what was to become one of the most important

moments of his life and his career, the love of young George's life dumped him. It was a heartsick teenager who was driving from his home in Barberton to his job in Wooster in the midst of World War II. Angry, upset, and filled with all the wounds that could be created by high-school love, the young singer began to wonder just how much he really meant to the girl whom he had once thought loved him. After considering all the times and ways the young woman had mistreated him, George decided that she prized the candy kisses her mother gave her more than those that came from his lips. This realization did more than just frustrate him, it inspired him.

Arriving at the radio studio early, Morgan sat down at a table and allowed a song to literally write itself. Within ten minutes he had not only finished the lyrics, but fully polished the music. With his guitar in hand, he premiered "Candy Kisses" live on the radio just moments after he had completed it. At that time the only real satisfaction he felt as he sang the song was that he had finally informed the selfish young lady just how he really felt about their relationship. Yet this simple song would not only open a succession of doors for him, it would put him in a spot where a generation later he could introduce the world to a daughter who would become even a larger star than her father.

Though he sang hillbilly music, George's smooth sound was far more pop than country. If he had come along at any other time, he probably would not have caught on with the hillbilly crowd. He simply wasn't cut out of the same mold as Ernest Tubb or Roy Acuff. And if not for the success of folks like Eddy Arnold and Red Foley, Morgan probably would have had to pursue a musical style on the outside of country. Yet because of the success that Eddy and Red were having in both country and pop singing traditional songs without much of a twang, a door opened up for Morgan not long after he left high school. The WWVA Jamboree, a very popular radio show out of Wheeling, West Virginia, needed a smooth country singer to offset the growing popularity of the Opry's Arnold, and so they called George and offered him a spot on their program. He accepted, packed his bags and moved to Wheeling. Once on the air, he introduced "Candy Kisses" to an audience that included listeners from most of the eastern portions of the nation. George and his "theme" song were a huge hit.

In short order, successful road dates and large bags of fan mail quickly made Morgan one of the show's biggest attractions. He become so big that even without a single hit record, he received an invitation to join the Opry in late 1948. Receiving an invitation to join the Opry without a big record was unheard of then as well as now and yet ironically Morgan's own daughter would also receive her invitation to join the Opry a generation later without a hit record.

His arrival in Nashville showed just how unprepared Morgan was for stardom. He had driven into town because he had been scheduled to appear on the Opry bill. Yet he didn't even know how to get to the show. As the minutes grew closer to his appearance time, he was lost downtown, walking frantically around looking for Ryman Auditorium. He finally stopped and asked a man on a street corner for directions. As he caught the gentleman's image in the street lights, Morgan realized that he had just met the man most responsible for opening the doors of country music to him, Eddy Arnold. Arnold not only showed George the way on that evening, but became a friend for life.

Just like he had done in Wheeling, Morgan rapidly charmed both the fans and the Opry's management. He also caught the eye of Columbia's talent scouts. Within a few months, the label had Morgan under contract and in the studio. Their foremost goal was getting George's theme song out in the marketplace.

Late in February "Candy Kisses" was shipped to radio stations and sales outlets from coast to coast. Columbia's leadership felt the record would do well, but in their wildest dreams they just couldn't have guessed how well. By the first of April, Morgan had placed his first single at number one. He would register three weeks at the top and keep "Candy Kisses" on the charts for twenty-three weeks. It would be his all-time biggest hit and would quickly become one of country music's most covered records.

Five other country music acts cut "Candy Kisses" in just 1949. These artists, Elton Britt, Red Foley, Cowboy Copas, Eddie Kirk, and Bud Hobbs, all planted their records in the top twenty. The first four acts even went to top-ten status. All together, the six country cuts of "Candy Kisses" spent sixty-five weeks on the charts.

On the pop side, Eddy Howard & His Orchestra quickly noted Morgan's country cut. They hurried to the studio to engineer a big band version of the song. By late spring, Howard's version had jumped "Candy Kisses" into the top twenty.

In country music's long and proud history, there have been a host of novelty or gimmick songs that have done well on the charts. A few rose above their own catchy titles and novel lyrics to become something special. Hank Thompson's "Humpty Dumpty Heart" was one of these. Another was "So Round, So Firm, So Fully Packed" by Merle Travis. Many, such as Tex Williams' "Smoke! Smoke! Smoke!" or the Bellamy Brothers' "If I Said You Had A Beautiful Body, Would You Hold It Against Me?" were chart-busting smashes, but still had little going for them other than their gimmicks. Most other novelty numbers were forgotten almost as quickly as they had been written and produced. Yet of all of the songs that fit into this special category, George Morgan's story of high school romance stands apart and made the singer/ songwriter a star.

"Candy Kisses" became more than a gimmick because you didn't even have to know what candy kisses were to fall in love with the song. At least two million copies were pressed and sold, and the single's success paved the way for George to sing it around the world. It also gave him the foundation he needed for a long career doing something he really loved—performing!

Morgan, who was often billed as "The Country Boy with the Velvet Voice," was so popular that Dinah Shore and Rosemary Clooney requested that he do duets with them for pop music releases. He also hosted a television program and became the first country music performer to sing with a major symphony. Yet for Morgan it wasn't the long list of hits that caused his chest to swell with pride, after all that was simply what he did for a living, what really made him proud was his lovely wife Anna, and their five children, Candy (named after his first hit song), Bethany, Liana, Matthew Martin (or Marty, after his good friend Marty Robbins), and Loretta Lynn.

Today most people naturally assume that Lorrie was named for country music superstar, Loretta Lynn. While Lynn and her father did become friends, at the time Lorrie was born, the "Coal Miner's Daughter" hadn't made it to Nashville or met Opry star George Morgan. The future Hall of Famer was simply an unknown mother. Hence, Lorrie was simply given her name because her parents thought it suited her. Later wearing the handle of Loretta Lynn was a bit of foreshadowing that couldn't help but be noted by not only the country music fans, but by Ms. Morgan too. In every way Lorrie seemed to have star written on every facet of her life.

In the homes of most entertainers, it is the parent who stays home that bonds most closely with the children. Certainly this was true with second generation country stars such as Pam Tillis. Pam rarely spent much time with Mel. Yet in Lorrie and her siblings' cases, it was different. While it was true that George was absent a great deal playing road dates, that didn't mean that he didn't take an active interest in his family. When he was home, he found a lot of time to spend with all his kids. Whatever their interest was, he would take the moments to become a part of it with them. In Lorrie's case, this often meant going out on the porch with guitars and singing songs until she wore out. That sometimes meant hours of trading licks and choruses.

Lorrie had sung since she could talk, and at five she had a long list of tunes she would sing upon command. She had watched her father enough in the spotlight to realize that you got a lot of attention if you could sing well. So whenever she got the chance, the youngest Mor-

gan would belt out everything from a country standard
to the latest Beatles hit. Her sisters would even help Lorrie organize family shows and hold flashlights from the
Morgans' stairs to spotlight the small girl who was so
desperately trying to impress her daddy. As she grew
more confident, Lorrie had her mother cut her hair in a
Beatles mop-look and she charged admission before singing her heart out to something like Petula Clark's
"Downtown." In her pre-school mind, she was already
Lorrie Morgan "star." And that attitude impressed her
father.

George, who could see that his little girl had talent,
encouraged Lorrie to learn new songs, as well as pick up
piano and guitar, but he never pushed her. If she wanted
to be a singer, that was fine, but he knew just how hard
the work was and the price every country music artist
had to pay to be a success. He only wanted his daughter
to pay that price if she really wanted to.

And even though she couldn't fully comprehend it,
even at a young age Lorrie had to understand a little bit
about how high that price was. She saw how much her
father hated to leave on long road trips. She watched him
pull out of the driveway with four or five other men,
crowded into a car, their instruments strapped on a lug-
gage rack. She even knew how tired he was when the
long trips were finished. Yet she also realized just how
much George loved performing and how much energy he
received when the fans reached out to him with words
of encouragement, cheers and cries for more. These re-
actions seemed to make the hard work worth any price!
And young Lorrie had to have dreamed of creating this
kind of excitement herself. So if becoming an entertainer
had been a disease, Lorrie had caught the bug before she
had attended a single day of school, and it was almost
all because her father was a part of the business.

At five Lorrie began to tag along with George when
he worked local shows. Because she loved to sing, she
even appeared and sang with her father from time to time
on WSM-TV's early morning live show. This was a program that featured many of Nashville's best-known coun-

try acts, and little Miss Morgan was getting to know them in a very special way—as a performing peer. Soon Lorrie was being used so often at WSM that she was getting small paychecks for singing on the air. As the years went by, the dates increased. By the time she was in junior high school, Lorrie was there almost every time her father appeared.

"Dad would take me to the *Morning Show* and then he'd take me to school," Morgan later recalled when speaking of her early career. And for Lorrie those days with her father were treasured times. If any memory of her youth stood out as being extra special, it had to be her father sharing the spotlight with her. And those moments seemed to charm everyone.

Yet even though she seemed like the ideal little girl in public, Lorrie was not perfect. She was not demure. If anything, she was demanding. She wanted her way and she wasn't afraid to make sure that folks knew it. George called his daughter Lorrie in public, but as she grew and it became obvious that she had been born with an argumentative spirit, he soon referred to her as "Fussy" when they were out of the spotlight. Lorrie would tell Jack Hurst of the *St. Paul Pioneer Press* in 1984 that the name fit. "I argued about everything all the time and was never satisfied." The latter quality would drive her to seeking perfection when she finally was given her own real shot at stardom, and it would contribute mightily to putting her career on solid ground.

While it may have been hard to satisfy the pretty little girl in matters of what she was going to eat or where she was going to get to go, she was completely satisfied with who she was. She never denied her country roots. And while many other children of Opry stars tried to distance themselves from country music, Lorrie didn't. Many times this stubborn pride created problems for her. In grade school, kids often made fun of Lorrie for being a hillbilly. They didn't think going to the Opry was cool. Lorrie told Hugh Wyatt of the New York *Daily News* some twenty-five years later, "I was always too strong-headed to let it shame me. I just wanted to beat somebody up.''

Yet when she was on the road with her dad the opposite kind of attention came her way. Country music fans everywhere fawned over her because she was the daughter of a star. Everyone made a big deal out of her for being an Opry performer's daughter. It didn't take Lorrie long to figure out that being George Morgan's baby meant something special. She could move to the front of the line, get free drinks and popcorn, and sit in the best seat. People even wanted to take her picture, get her autograph, and listen to her sing. On the road she was a little star because her dad was such a big star. And she ate it up.

Yet Lorrie's real appreciation for her father and his work was based on more than just feeling special because people fussed over his pretty little kid. Everywhere she turned she could see fans and performers who revered George Morgan. She also quickly discovered that almost everyone could sing his classic hit ''Candy Kisses.'' Simply put, even in her young eyes, she knew that her daddy wasn't like everyone else's daddy. There were a lot of people who thought he was very special. And probably because of that fact, she watched everything he did intently. He quickly became not only her father, but her hero and mentor.

''He was absolutely the smoothest man on stage,'' she would later say time and time again. ''You never knew he had a nerve in his body. He talked slow and so easy, and everybody understood everything he said.''

Lorrie also noted that as George joked with the audience, he got to know them by letting them really get to know him as a person. He didn't put on, he talked about his life, shared his dreams, and made everyone feel as if they were special. And best of all he really did enjoy what he was doing. And when it came the time when he would sing ''Candy Kisses,'' the audience would always fall apart.

Everyone knew ''Candy Kisses,'' and most of the crowds who cheered so hard when George began to sing that ballad, would sing it with him. To Lorrie it seemed that everyone in the world had heard the song and knew who her father was.

"It sold millions and millions of records both here and overseas," Lorrie would later explain about that special song and why she loved not only it, but what her father did for a living. "Now if your dad had a number-one smash country hit wouldn't you develop somewhat of an interest in music?" And as she grew from a cute little girl into a beautiful teen, so too grew her appreciation of her father's brand of music.

Yet country wasn't all that Lorrie listened to. At home her older brother and sisters got Lorrie into the Supremes, Dionne Warwick, the Eagles, and Led Zeppelin. On her own, she developed an appreciation for Johnny Mathis and Karen Carpenter. She would sing anything she liked, and she seemed to like music from every entertainment genre. Yet by and large, unlike other country music daughters like Pam Tillis and Carlene Carter, even as a child it was country music that meant the most to Lorrie. Rock was all right, but rock didn't have the Opry and rock stars didn't seem to be real people. In country music there was an honesty that the young girl didn't see anywhere else. This was probably due in large part to how honest her father had been with her, her family, their friends and his fans, as well as how wonderful all of the other stars treated George's little girl.

When Lorrie first began to travel to shows with George, he had told her to never say never and always mind her manners. So even though she had a mind of her own and a driving and fiery spirit, she tried to be as nice as her father was. From an early age, she understood that the Morgan name meant something special to Music City. People respected it and she didn't want to do anything to mess up what her father had so carefully built and so earnestly guarded. Hence, because she was so proud to be George's daughter—the daughter of a country music singer—she was almost always immediately loved by every one of the show business folks who met her. Yet more than just loved and fawned over, Lorrie was taken under wing and let inside the inner circle even as a grade school student because she so loved their music. And when this happened, she became not just the child of an Opry star, but an Opry kid.

Because of this inner circle status, Lorrie grew up really getting to know the women of country music. They gave her advice, taught her songs, told her stories, and shared the glamorous side of show business with her. These figures, such as Jeannie Shepard, Jeannie Pruett, Connie Smith, and a host of others were her "aunts." They kept up with what she was doing and encouraged her to seek out her dreams. And how she watched them. As these women charmed audiences with their big hair and glittery outfits, she took note. She observed carefully as these Opry stars put on their make-up and even though it might have been heavy enough to suit a streetwalker, in Lorrie's mind it was perfectly applied. Lorrie noted that their shoes matched their dresses, and that they always cared enough to take the time to present themselves and their music in a way that fans would remember. And they always gave the crowd a piece of their hearts. They truly cared about their fans and wanted to give them something special everytime they took centerstage.

As she watched from the back of the stage, Lorrie seemed to feel as if she needed to be basking in that warm spotlight. She also seemed to realize that her home was on the stage of the Grand Ole Opry and her extended family was here too. And on Saturday nights as George Morgan sang "Candy Kisses" to families who had driven hundreds or even thousands of miles just to catch him on this stage and at this moment, music became so much more than a business and her father became so much more than just a recording artist. Lorrie must have realized even then that music was something very special and George Morgan was something special because he could use that music and touch people's hearts. And this was something that she would always remember, because her father gave her moments that she and her fans could never forget!

Chapter 2

By the time she was in junior high Lorrie wanted to spend more time at her father's shows than she did anywhere else. The fact was that while other kids were having slumber parties, going to dances, playing ball, or hanging out at the soda shop or mall, when she was given a choice, Lorrie was usually backstage with her dad. And while she was there she was getting to know the business from set up to take down. She understood everything from sound checks to feedback. She knew more about running lights and sound boards than most drama majors in college. She was good at running sales too. And as a salesperson, she could easily talk fans into buying her father's tapes and records. She could also smile, laugh, and joke with the most seasoned fan or performer in a manner that made her appear much older than her years.

By the same token, Lorrie also understood that this was not just a glamour business. She saw the work it took to pull equipment up on stage. She knew how long it took to break in a new musician. Lorrie had been around country music enough to recognize just how tough most of the stars had it. Even those who were making big money had very little time to enjoy it, and, in truth, there just weren't that many country music performers who were making "big" money. Yet most of the entertainers she knew gave and gave and gave without ever complaining. And as she watched firsthand these stars give back to their fans, it made a deep impression on her. Morgan never forgot the sacrifices the genre's pioneers made and what these sacrifices meant to the fans.

In 1991 Lorrie told Ed Bumgardner of the *Winston-*

Salem Journal, ''The business was tougher (when her father had worked the road making his career). The road was terrible; performers had to leave their families and tour constantly to make ends meet. And performers didn't ride around in Silver Eagle buses. They drove themselves, crammed together in cars, often driving in shifts round the clock.''

The youngest Morgan was well aware that her father's tours were scatter-shot at best. He might be in New England on a Tuesday, in a small town in Illinois on a Wednesday, and in Florida on a Thursday. During this whole run the band might never get to sleep in a bed and they almost always had to eat their meals on the go. Worn-out and rundown, they nevertheless had to play to crowds who wanted to see them at their best. And those crowds almost always did. Then the stars who cared for the fans like Lorrie's father did would stay and sign autographs and pose for pictures until they cut it so close they barely had time to make it to the next date and set up.

Even at this young age, Lorrie was smart enough to know that a lot of the pain and heartache that was such an important part the great country music songs came from the life the performers had to live. Many marriages didn't survive. A host of entertainers turned to booze and drugs to cope with the stress and strain. Scores of stars lost touch with their families and themselves while they were staying in touch with the fans and radio jocks. In their quest for fame and fortune, they burned their candles at both ends.

The young child knew the stories of Hank Williams, Lefty Frizzell, and the others who had turned to the bottle to escape their lives. She also knew all about how Patsy Cline, Jim Reeves, Johnny Horton, and so many others had died en route to another show. She had not only heard the stories, but she had seen firsthand that the cost of this crazy life was high—too high for most. And yet Lorrie didn't fear that cost because her dad had handled it all so well.

George Morgan had sold out scores of theaters, but he

had never sold out his soul. Even in the midst of a life of one-night stands and long road tours, he had stayed true to himself and his family. While others had drunk, he fought off the fatigue with laugher and stories of looking forward to getting home. When others had strayed with some easy woman whose goal in life was to sleep with a country music star, he had called home and visited on the phone with his beloved Anna. That fact was that George had faced the temptations and kept his priorities in line. For that big reason, he was the best possible role model for a little girl who wished for nothing better than getting a chance to share a stage with her father.

Morgan loved to show his youngest off too. He was proud to present her to an audience at his concerts and George looked forward to getting Lorrie a chance to perform on WSM-TV also. He not only knew she could handle this pressure, but that she would do well too. He somehow sensed that she had what it took to handle this business and come out on top. Still, there would be no pressure on his part for Lorrie to become a performer because he knew that the only way to enter show business was with a strong desire in your heart and your head focused on the many high prices you had to pay to make your career work. So he didn't force her into it. He waited to see signs from her. If she wanted to perform, he let her tell him with her words or actions. And she told him time and time again that she wanted her shot at the spotlight.

Yet in order to really feature Lorrie, in order to really find out if she wanted to give country music a real shot, George knew that that there was only one stage that offered a real test. Lorrie knew that stage well. She had practically grown up there. She was friends with everyone from the stagehands to the announcer. But knowing every board and nail wasn't enough. Having walked those boards when the lights were down wasn't enough either. Being ready for the Opry spotlight was something far different than being able to sing on a radio show or knowing your way around the building. It took a combination of guts, guile, and experience.

A host of veteran entertainers had fallen apart under the pressure of performing at the Opry. The show's management had even suggested to Elvis that he go back to driving trucks after his dismal debut on the Ryman stage. And Presley had been young man who had been seasoned for the big show by clubs and road dates. So as much as George wanted to give his daughter a chance to perform with her "musical family," he also didn't want to push her out there before she could handle it. Her wanted her to be able to look back on her Opry debut as a successful and happy moment.

Lorrie and her father had talked about singing a song on the Opry for some time. Many of the regular performers had urged them on. Most felt that a father/daughter duet would be perfect. Yet Morgan didn't see a duet as the avenue for a young lady who had proven to him that she could do well on her own. When he finally decided that she was old enough, he wanted Lorrie to get to have the spotlight to herself. One day, when Lorrie was just fourteen, the time seemed right. George came off the road and asked Lorrie if she would like to be a part of the upcoming Saturday Opry show. Her heart must have skipped more than just a beat as she enthusiastically responded.

So while she had been singing in public since she was five, Lorrie's career really began at the age of fourteen. Here is when she naturally jumped at the chance to sing at the Opry. Then, after the giddiness of walking on the hallowed stage left, the reality of the situation hit her. She was not going to be going to the Ryman as a fan, she would be there as a performer. This would not be just another trip to watch the show, on this night she would be there to work the show. Suddenly sick to her stomach with worry, she couldn't wait to get downtown and work with the staff players on an old country standard. When that time came and the seasoned veterans who had played for the likes of Hank Williams and Marty Robbins had gotten the tracks of Lorrie's number straight, the bold and very young teen, though racked with stagefright, asked what song she should do if she received a call for an encore. The pros who were working with her on the arrangement simply laughed and told her not to worry about it, no one ever got enough applause to do an encore anymore. Then, not wanting to scare her, they added that if she did, then she should just do the same song again. That was what Hank Williams had done when he had debuted, and if it was good enough for Hank, they reasoned, then it had to be good enough to George Morgan's little girl too.

As time crept by, Lorrie wasn't the only one nervous on that 1974 evening. George would tell his friends after the show, "If a performer thinks they get stagefright before they perform, wait until their child makes their first performance, and you are waiting and watching."

Yet for Lorrie it had to be worse. Act after act got their chance, as she waited. Star after star stood in the wings and wished her well, then did their own thing. Time and time again she glanced in the mirror to check the simple but pretty dress that she and her mother had chosen for this special occasion. Again and again she ran over the lyrics in her head. She must have checked the time on the clock on the wall a hundred times. Then, after what seemed like days, it was time for George Morgan's part of the show. As she watched her long, lean father stroll on stage, Lorrie had to have been scared to death. Yet those around her didn't notice. To most of them Lorrie looked as if she had been born for this moment. What poise, they thought.

A decade later Lorrie told writer Jack Hurst about an "out" clause that she and her father had worked out just before he had gone on. The singer explained that, "Before Dad went out onto the stage he said, 'Just before I introduce you, I'll look over at you, and if you're too nervous and don't want to come out, just shake your head.'"

When it came time for her number, her father glanced over at her waiting in the wings. As he looked into her beautiful eyes, he must have seen her resolve. She was ready. She wanted to go on and was ready to try to charm the crowd. He could see that, and it must have warmed his heart. There would be no "out" clause used this evening. Turning back to the audience he then explained that a member of his family was about to make her Opry debut. After a father's proud introduction, he turned the stage over to the pretty little girl who couldn't wait to sing her song.

Lorrie would recall, "He introduced me. I walked out and stood in one spot. Never moved. Never even looked at anybody. But in the corner of my eye, I could see Dad standing there just bawling."

On a night when her father had introduced her to his favorite crowd at his favorite place, the teen won the hearts of the packed house with her version of "Paper Roses." When she finished singing, the crowd rose to their feet, thus marking the first standing ovation at the Opry in more than a dozen years. It seemed that neither Lorrie nor the crowd realized that she had sung the second verse twice. And if anyone did, it didn't matter. Her voice had been strong beyond her years. Her eyes had shown with star-power that hid her own lack of confidence. And her personality had beamed so brightly that she didn't even need a spotlight. And when she had finished, how the crowd had come alive.

How many performers had come and gone at the Ryman without ever receiving a standing ovation? The number had to have been in the hundreds, maybe the thousands. The names which had debuted there at the Opry to only a simple round of applause were some of the top names in the business. And while the audiences had generally been warm to each of them, none of them in more than a decade had been received like this. The only way to quiet the screaming masses was with an encore, so Lorrie followed the shocked band's lead and launched into another verse of "Paper Roses," and the crowd's vocal bouquets continued.

Backstage stars were popping out of dressing rooms to catch what was happening on the hallowed Ryman stage. The wings filled with musicians who wanted to watch history. The giants of the old show were there shaking their heads and smiling. A few might have even been a bit jealous. None would have predicted it. And for the next few weeks, Lorrie's debut would be the most spoken of topic of conversation at the Grand Ole Opry.

"When it was over," Lorrie remembered, "and those people gave me a standing ovation, I thought 'This is what I'm doing the rest of my life.' I thought it was going to be easy. Little did I know."

Of course at that moment it did seem easy and it was fun, yet in all honesty, the fun was just beginning. And the hard work was just beginning too. And Lorrie knew all about that work too. She had seen it firsthand and it hadn't scared her. Besides the standing ovations made it worth it.

"I think I was pretty well destined for it (the music business)," Morgan would later explain time and time again. "I think whether I wanted to or not, it was kind of in my blood and something I didn't have a choice of doing. I was always in it. I was always there. It was all I knew growing up. So whether it would have been the entertainment end of it or behind the scenes, I think I would have been in it somehow."

Yet this moment in the Opry spotlight had to have been the turning point. It had to have cinched her desire to be a performer. She would later tell the Associated Press, "I knew then that that's what I wanted to do from that moment on." For Lorrie there was no longer a question of *if*, now she knew that this was her destiny.

Most unenlightened fans probably assumed that from that night on, Lorrie's life was much different than it had been before. After all, how many performers began their careers in such an incredible manner? In reality Lorrie's life changed hardly at all. She still went to school, still did her homework, still had chores around the house, and was still the baby sister. Yet at home and at the Opry, these were happy times. The Morgans were together, George was spending a bit more time at home, and in the midst of a world seemingly gone mad with presidents resigning in scandal and riots and demonstrations in big cities and on university campuses, the Morgan home was settled, secure, and peaceful. This was a tribute to the fact that even though George was a star, he never had a star's mentality. His home was a place where a husband and father lived with his wife and children, not an address where a "star" reigned.

The family's Christmases were classic examples of just how wonderful life was for Lorrie and her family. George was always home, the tree was always perfect, the family never forgot the reason for the season and always went to Mass, and presents were always there waiting. Some time on every Christmas Eve, everyone also knew that George would bring out his guitar and sing songs. A Christmas couldn't go by without his personal favorite, "Silent Night." And so with Lorrie now a seasoned Opry performer, George had a family co-star to debut with him.

No one could have known and certainly no one would have predicted that 1974 would have been the last Christmas that country music's perfect family would have together. Just like no one would have guessed that easy-going George, the man who always seemed to take care of himself, the performer who hadn't gotten involved in the excesses of show business, the man who didn't lie, cheat, or lose himself in a bottle, would be a walking timebomb either.

On May 26, 1975, George was installing a television antenna on the family home, when a heart attack suddenly hit him like a nine-pound hammer. He had been rushed to Nashville's Baptist Hospital and doctors had managed to get him stabilized. Yet there wasn't much more that they could do. Open-heart surgery was still in its experimental stages and was only attempted in very severe cases. For the country music star, the prescription was therefore simply rest and medicine. He also needed to cut back on his hectic lifestyle and many of his road dates. All things considered, though he appeared weak and frail, most of the people around the Morgans sensed that he could continue to live a productive and long life.

On June 28, George was back on the Opry where he celebrated his birthday with his fans doing what he loved to do most, performing. Yet in truth, he had probably rushed things too much. Though the applause and cheers had lifted his spirits, he didn't feel well. Within a few days he was rushed back to the hospital. Now his heart was really giving him troubles. With his condition growing worse, the doctors felt that the only chance Morgan had was to employ the rarely used bypass surgery. Performed the first week in July, the surgery was simply too little, too late. Within days of the operation George had lapsed into unconsciousness and on Monday, July 7, he passed away in his bed at Baptist Hospital. His smooth voice had been stilled for the final time.

Most of the movers and shakers in country music, as well as the members and staff of the Opry, were at his funeral mass at St. Joseph's Catholic Church. Greeting reporters and family members, Johnny Cash spoke for the entire country music community when he sincerely noted that "George Morgan never had a selfish, self-centered thought in his life. He was a man of charity, a man of love. His first concern was always his home and family."

Cash's wife, June Carter, added, "I'll remember George as one of the truest, finest gentlemen I've ever known in my life."

Like most of those attending this tragic funeral, the Cashes were moved to tears on several occasions. No one seemed to be able to come to grips with the fact that one of the nicest stars country music had ever known had simply left life's stage so soon. At the next Opry show, scores of people kept asking, "Why?"

Yet in truth, no one should have been surprised. Morgan had always given so much to everyone else, especially his fans, that he probably hadn't kept enough for himself. He had also given from his heart so easily, so no one could have known just what it was taking from him. The road, coupled with all those hours he could have been resting but instead was out there autographing and visiting, had taken its toll on George. And his daughter Lorrie, more than most, knew that even if he hadn't abused drugs or alcohol, just making a living in this business meant going without sleep, working three and four shows a day, and doing things that a human body just couldn't do for very long without collapsing. So thousands of others may have asked how this could have happened, but Lorrie had to have known. George gave and gave and gave. Eventually there just wasn't anything left to give. Still, it simply wasn't fair.

Her father's death hit Lorrie hard. She had lost more than a dad, she had lost a mentor and guide. He had made her dreams possible, he had opened the doors, he had given her the advice and he had taught her the lessons. He was supposed to be there beside her as she built her career and life. He was supposed to be a grandfather to her children. To give her away at the altar. Yet even though he wouldn't be able to do those things, in death his influence over his daughter was still strong. His performances and his words echoed in her head. Rather than letting her dream of performing die when her father was buried, she was determined to keep it alive so that his name and place in country music would be remembered. She didn't want the world to forget George Morgan, not for a second. The best way she could see to do that was to show the world what he had taught her.

So Lorrie went to work learning new songs and meeting with her father's band members. She wanted them to stay together and hit the road with the teenager in front of them. Most agreed to give it a try and a few dates were put together.

"My dad always told me they can hear you sing on the radio," Lorrie explained, and she could still work on WSM any time she wanted. "Yet when they come to a concert they like to get to know you a little bit." With her father's band supporting her, Lorrie decided that it was time for country music to really get to know her.

The fact that Lorrie was going to work a few dates was soon not the only news that would put Ms. Morgan's name out in front of the masses. More than a few record executives were mulling over signing her to a record contract. First of all, her Opry appearances had proven she could sing and had the crowd presence a successful artist needed. Secondly, she was not only talented, but cute too! She was also well-connected. Everyone in the business knew her. And finally there was a bit of morbid fan interest that could be cashed in because of George's unexpected death. In other words, there were folks who sensed that a dollar could be made by using Lorrie to get to the pocketbooks of the late star's fans.

Death often revived careers. This had happened time and time again. Yet most record companies couldn't see their way clear to using Lorrie to help them make a few bucks off of George's passing. For starters, George hadn't been in the top ten since 1960, had not been a part of the hot new generation of country stars, and the labels had statistics that proved that now most Opry stars were simply not getting a big dollar response at the cash register. So the bottom line seemed to say that while Morgan's fans had been loyal to him and that they loved him, the numbers weren't there to justify putting much money into his unproven teenage daughter. Yet Four Star, a company that had recently signed George and had released his last two singles, went against this thinking.

On August 5, 1975, less than a month after George had died, the *Nashville Banner* played out the following headline, "Lori Morgan to Sign Record Pact." The article, complete with a misspelling of Lorrie's first name, written by Red O'Donnell, began, "Lori Morgan, sixteen-year-old daughter of George and Anna Morgan, is going to follow in the tuneful tracks of her late father."

At the time Lorrie was a high school junior at St. Bernard Academy (a private Catholic high school). Joe Johnson, a Music Row veteran and owner of Four Star Music Publishing Company and the independent, Four Star Records, announced the deal, indicating that Lorrie would be in the studio within the week.

"This was no spur-of-the-moment decision," said Bob Jennings, Four Star's vice president, in the company's press release. "We talked with her and George several times in the past. We heard her sing at the Grand Ole Opry and on an Opryland show. She is a fine singer—and has a winning personality."

Bob Jennings added it wasn't simply turned onto the

young woman's ability to sing. He added, "Additionally, she had the potential to be a hit songwriter. In fact we plan to record one she wrote with the help of her older brother (Marty). It's called 'A Child's Dream.' "

Johnson also felt that he would want to record another original tune called "Walking in My Daddy's Shadow."

"She had a fresh sound, a fresh, clean look," said Jennings. "I really think she had the makings of a star."

Lorrie told the press, "Daddy and I discussed my career as an entertainer-writer several times. He suggested that I get an education and then give more thought to my career. As things are now, I'm going to school—and see if I can become a professional singer-writer too. You might say that I am going to try to pick up where my Daddy left off."

Unlike other labels who had looked at Lorrie in the days after her father's death, Four Star had been there for almost a year. They had talked with her father about her on several occasions. They had seen Lorrie as a possible rival for the hot new country music child star Tanya Tucker.

Tucker had been tearing up the country charts for more than three years. Tanya, a year older than Lorrie, had debuted on the playlists in 1972. In the time that had followed she had topped the charts four times for Columbia and was now signing a big new contract with MCA. She was being featured on network television shows and being interviewed by the biggest names in the media too. Tanya was country music's first big teen idol.

Four Star thought that Lorrie had everything that Tanya had and was starting her recording career with a bit more in the bank. The label also believed that Lorrie was cuter, just as talented as Tucker, and had a name that meant something special to country music fans. Lorrie's career could be launched, they therefore reasoned, with a readymade Morgan fan base. To Johnson and Jennings and a few so-called experts, it seemed that she was in the right place at the right time, and that Four Star had the right formula to make it all work to her advantage.

Yet while Lorrie had seen country music through her

father's shows, she hadn't had the chance to live it through her own. When she began to live the grind of a struggling performer, she realized that she hadn't been as prepared as she had once thought she was. She also realized that she was no longer the innocent teenager who could easily hang with her schoolmates.

She later told Jim Washburn of the *Los Angeles Times,* "In school I sometimes felt I didn't have much in common with the other kids. While they were doing their homework and stuff, I was singing in nightclubs, dealing with drunks, and trying to make my way in the music business."

The drunk men who wanted her in ways that the nuns in the Catholic schools didn't speak about, the smoky rooms and the sparse crowds, the fact that many cared more about their drinks than the music, and the nights of little sleep, quickly showed young Lorrie that this was a life that wasn't for everyone. The applause was earned, not freely given, and at the starting point of a career, there wasn't much adulation. Many, including some who watched her grow up at the Opry, figured that she wouldn't last too long before deciding to head back to a life that centered on homework, slumber parties, and dating. Yet if they had known Lorrie well they would have realized that she wouldn't give up easily. She was, after all, doing this for more than just herself. She was doing this for her father too! Turning her back on a music career meant that she would lose a part of his influence and his death would become more real, and she wasn't ready for that. Unfortunately, as the next few months would clearly show, she wasn't ready for the big time yet either.

Chapter 3

Nashville was moving to a new sound by the last half of the seventies. This sound, spurred on later by the *Urban Cowboy* movement, was known at first as country-politan. Three artists who were extremely successful in riding this more pop-oriented Nashville music to the top of the charts were Ronnie Milsap, Eddie Rabbitt, and Barbara Mandrell.

Rabbitt was a city-born Easterner who had moved to Nashville as a songwriter. His first real break came when Elvis Presley scored a hit with an Eddie-penned tune, "Kentucky Rain." By 1976 Rabbitt had taken "Drinkin' My Baby Off of My Mind" to the top of the country charts. He would follow that with a series of number one's including "You Don't Love Me Anymore," "Every Which Way but Loose," and "Drivin' My Life Away." Dark, rugged and handsome, he was a country music hunk before the term had even been invented.

Ronnie Milsap was an even more charismatic figure than Rabbitt. A blind singer/pianist, he had first hit the charts in 1973 at the age of twenty-seven, and a year later earned his first chart topper with "Pure Love," a song written by Eddie Rabbitt. Milsap, who was energetic and funny, took off from there to earn a shelf full of number one's, including "Please Don't Tell Me How the Story Ends," "Daydreams About Night Things," and the classic "Only One Love in My Life."

Barbara Mandrell, the new female force in country music, had been around the business since about the time that Lorrie Morgan was born. She had worked her way up through the ranks as a steel player and child stage sensation on the west coast. Barely five feet tall, she was beautiful, extremely talented, and driven. She was also savvy. When producer Tom Collins began spinning hit sessions for her at ABC/Dot, and later at MCA, she became the dominant entertainer in Music City. Mandrell's songs might not have been considered classics by the Music City elite, but the fans ate up "Woman to Woman," "Sleeping Single in a Double Bed," and "Crackers." Other women could still chart, and many like Crystal Gayle did put out a long list of hits, but Mandrell owned the entertainment side of the business. Unlike past "gal" artists who had come up as mere opening acts for men, she closed the shows. She would be the role model for folks like Reba McEntire and the next generation of country music women.

Yet while Barbara was quickly working her way up the ladder from county fairs to sold-out auditoriums, Lorrie Morgan was struggling to be heard. At about the same time as her high-school graduation, Lorrie was being showcased at Nashville's Ramada Inn Airport as a Monday night feature performer. It wasn't exactly a big gig, but at least fans who had come to town to catch Nashville's spin on the world could see a star's daughter for a fair price.

Four Star, which had yet to generate much enthusiasm for Lorrie's recording career, was watching her from a distance. Like many in Nashville, they were waiting to see if the now beautiful woman/child was ever going to break out with the fans. Now, almost two years after her father's death, many were simply writing her off as a novelty.

Yet there was one place where the people still appreciated her, and that was the Opry. Whenever the show needed a guest to fill in on short notice, they knew that they could count on Lorrie. And though she was no longer receiving standing ovations, she was still a fan favorite. Yet when Lorrie had asked and then later begged the Opry to become a regular member, the old show had backed off. She didn't have a hit record, and they felt that she needed that to establish herself as an act.

The fact that she was a favorite guest on the Opry might just have hurt her on the record side. The new stars, the Mandrells, Milsaps, and Rabbitts, didn't belong to the Opry. As a matter of fact, the grand old showcase was now largely looked upon as an icon from another era. A retirement home for performers who were out of style and could no longer draw on the road. For that matter, it wasn't cool to run with Porter and Little Jimmy, and if you did, then you just weren't pop enough to get a real record deal. Music City had gone Hollywood and Vegas and left hillbilly and corn pone behind.

At about the time Tanya headed to Los Angeles to go rock and Dolly crossed over to go pop, it would have seemed that Lorrie probably should have distanced herself from her roots too. More than a few gave her that advice. Yet she wouldn't do it. She loved the Opry and she believed that it was the home of real country music. The rest of the world could do what they wanted, but she was staying at home, even if staying at home meant working smoky clubs filled with a lot of very lonely and sad people and having the fans of the day's hot acts of today think she was anything but cool.

Wherever she played, the pretty brunette (the color would lighten later) was almost always co-billed with Little Roy Wiggins, a well-known steel guitar player. Wiggins had worked with some great folks in his decades in the business. The Nashville native had been a mainstay with Eddy Arnold's band for years, but he had actually joined the Opry in 1940 at the tender age of fourteen with Paul Howard's Arkansas Cotton Pickers. He had met Eddy when he had served a stint with Pee Wee King. It was Little Roy's steel that fans heard on such great tunes as "Bouquet of Roses," "Anytime," and "No Wings on My Angel." For almost three decades Wiggins worked with no one but Eddy, with the exception of one session with George Morgan in the late fifties. That bit of freelance work turned out a hit too. "I'm in Love Again."

When Little Roy left Eddy in the late sixties, he turned out a few solo albums and then joined George Morgan.

He would work with the "Candy Man" on many sessions and at a host of bookings. Hence, he was familiar with Lorrie. He had basically watched her grow up.

So fans of the late George Morgan were turning out to see not only the the budding star his daughter promised to become, but also the hot licks of a man they had followed for years. For the Ramada and other small venues it seemed like a promising combination.

By and large, even though Lorrie worked well with Wiggins and the other members of her father's band, the chemistry and timing just didn't seem to be right. The little girl who wanted to follow in her daddy's footsteps was having a difficult time making it in a town where the rules and music were changing rapidly.

Though making music was foremost on her mind, by 1977 Lorrie was best-known for her outstanding looks. Though small, at five foot two, she was perfectly proportioned, had been blessed with movie star beauty, and had poise beyond her years. Hence, it came as no surprise when Lorrie was named first runner-up in the Miss Nashville Beauty Pageant. Many felt that only her short stature kept her from walking away with the top honor. Still, for a few moments, the press played up the fact that George's youngest had almost taken home the crown. For Lorrie it became quickly apparent that first runner up wasn't good enough to take her any further than where she was, and a girl who wanted to make it in music didn't seem to have much use for college, so Morgan hit the streets and knocked on doors looking for jobs that would get her closer to the business. She finally landed a position as a receptionist for Acuff-Rose Publishing Company.

Acuff-Rose was Nashville's largest music publisher. It had been an important part of the Music City business scene since the forties. Their stable of writers was the strongest in town, and they could make or break a performer by simply turning some of that talent loose during a session.

There is no doubt that Lorrie's last name and Opry experience helped her land the job. The fact that was she was also knowledgeable about the business and really good-looking (which boded well for anyone who wanted to be a receptionist) was a big plus too. Yet, the bonus that might have worked best for Lorrie was that she had a solid voice and could go into the studio after hours to sing on some of the publishing company's demo sessions. That strength alone gave her a leg up on everyone else and could quickly make her Acuff-Rose's most valuable new employee. This also put Lorrie right where she wanted to be too.

A host of Nashville's biggest stars had been first recognized through their demo work. One of these was Kitty Wells. She had cut the demo on "It Wasn't God Who Made Honky Tonk Angels," and had done it so well that Decca had released the demo as a single and given Kitty a new recording contract as well. "Angels" of course made history as the first number one by a female country artist. Bill Anderson had also been heard on demos before getting his big shot. So had Willie Nelson and Roger Miller. This seemed to be a perfect spot for Lorrie to catch the ear of producers who had passed over her in the past as being too young or just another star's child who wanted to be an artist.

Lorrie had also hoped that Acuff-Rose would quickly take note of her writing abilities as well. Here she was initially disappointed. Even though the company used her demos and liked her work in the office, other doors in Nashville didn't fly open and no one in house seemed too interested in Morgan's songwriting. Hence, musically speaking, gigs like the Ramada were about the only thing that was happening besides the occasional visits to the Opry for a guest spot.

By 1978 Lorrie's dates with her father's band were now few and far between and the Morgan tie with the group finally died. For three years George's daughter had tried to hold it all together, but she wasn't generating enough money to feed her musicians' families. Sadly, the old band members and the young woman parted company. As they did, many expected Morgan's country music career to wind down too. Yet Lorrie wasn't ready to give up. She was still working as a guest on the Opry from time to time, and she was still at Acuff-Rose, even if it was in a capacity less than what she had wished it was. Then just when it appeared like giving up and going to college to search for new career options might have been the smartest thing she could do, a glimmer of hope broke through. Finally Acuff-Rose took note of her writing.

"I started writing," she would later recall, "and I did a lot of demo sessions during my lunch hour and after work. Any time they asked me to do a demo, I would do it, and finally I got signed to Hickory Records, which was owned by Acuff-Rose."

Hickory Records had signed her after catching her working with country music's legendary pianist Floyd Cramer at a special dinner for Wesley Rose. The set that she did for the audience proved to many that the girl had some talent that the organization had overlooked. Yet, the unanswered question even as they signed Lorrie was how much were they willing to put up to assure the young woman had a real chance at some success.

Hickory was not RCA or MCA, but when they got behind a song, they could make a hit. They had done it several times in the past. And with access to a great deal of Acuff-Rose's material, there were hits to be had in the catalog. After mulling through their material for some time, in March of 1979, a nineteen-year-old Lorrie finally hit the charts with "Two People in Love."

Watching a new release is much like viewing a cloud in a spring sky. At first it might appear small, but you continue to watch thinking that the afternoon heat and humid conditions might lead to a building, that over time will grow into a storm. More often than not, the cloud floats away as quickly as it appears, but you watch it hoping that somehow it will grow into a much-needed rain.

"Two People in Love," ABC/Hickory #54041, was a little cloud that failed to grow much. The single spent five weeks in country music's top one hundred songs, peaking at just the seventy-fifth position. Far from the promising start on which Acuff-Rose had hoped, the release seemed to prove that there simply wasn't much future in working the recording career of George Morgan's daughter.

Yet three months later, MCA, which had bought out ABC, tried again. They took Lorrie's "Tell Me I'm Only Dreaming," and launched it for a summer-time audience. It lasted but three weeks and barely made the climb into the eighties. As far as the company was concerned, the experiment was over and Lorrie was released.

It seemed that the only time Lorrie could find any success on a record was when no one knew she was a part of the session. Lorrie had the satisfaction of hearing her voice go into the top twenty when she did an uncredited appearance on Freddy Weller's "Love Got in the Way." Yet this didn't pave the way for stardom either. "Love Got in the Way" only earned Lorrie a few dollars for session work.

Late in 1979, the all-but-forgotten Four Star Records company appeared back on the scene. They had noted the success that RCA had earned by coupling the late Jim Reeves' voice with other artists in studio manufactured duets. Four Star brought Lorrie in, used her voice, put it with her father's, and released "I'm Completely Satisfied With You," in November hoping to cash in on the same kind of feeling that RCA had done with Reeves. This song was the first time Lorrie had ever teamed with her father on a recording. It probably would have worked a few years before too, but country music was now caught in the throes of the cross-over fever and the outlaw sound. "I'm Completely Satisfied With You," was out of step with this trend and couldn't compete with "Mammas Don't Let Your Babies Grow Up to Be Cowboys" and "Sleeping Single in a Double Bed." It hit the playlists for only three weeks, never going any higher than number ninety-three. The lack of success of this warm, rich single seemed to indicate that country radio had little use for nostalgia, history, or much of anything that harkened back to country music's rich past. Many critics, who were horrified by what they considered the bubblegum sound of new country, even wondered if the great

Hank Williams could have managed to write and sing a hit in today's market.

Grabbing a hit at Four Star had been Lorrie's last hope of generating a record deal in the Music City of the time. She was simply too linked with another era for this one to accept her. She would have to wait for not just another chance, but another time when music evolved into something that had a different feel. Yet as she waited, she would also have to eat. To help her out, her mother pitched in as a cheerleader, best friend, and in some cases, driver.

When Lorrie was working, she was now basically on her own. She would travel thousands of miles by car, bring along one musician, use a local band, and sometimes discover things were so bad at the date, that she would cry before and after the show. With her mom at her side, she would then leave, hurting to the bone because of bad house bands and rude patrons, hit the road, travel thousands of more miles only to face the same kind of working conditions again.

She would later recall those lean times with a bit of pride. After all, she had to have been tough just to survive them. "I drove thousands of miles with just me and my mom," she explained. "There were times I couldn't get through a show without literally crying because the band was so bad." Yet she kept going and kept pushing.

Though her music career was going nowhere, it was getting in the way of her social life. Lorrie dated and thought she had fallen in love with a young man she had known in high school, Brad Fly. He even gave her an engagement ring for Christmas. For a year as she struggled to get a deal and make a go of her career, he would hang around. Finally Brad grew impatient, gave up, and told Lorrie that he simply couldn't handle the music business and the demands of her life. In all honesty, he was probably tired of watching her spin her wheels and he must have realized that he was never going to be the most important thing in her life. He would always take a back seat to her music.

As Lorrie moved into life as a beautiful young woman,

she experimented by spreading her wings and trying things that many people thought George's little girl would never do. She remembered these days in a *Washington Post* interview in 1993 as a time when she did "too much partying and too much drinking."

Lorrie may have partied a bit as she looked for herself in a Music City that seemed like anything but home, but even then she still maintained a sense of control. Never did she forget whose daughter she was and what her father's name stood for. He might have been gone, but she didn't want to embarrass his memory. Even in the bad times, she was proud to be George Morgan's daughter.

As Lorrie roamed Nashville's hot spots and met new folks, it was only natural that those she spent the most time with were musicians. With folks who made their money and lived their dreams in the business, she felt a kinship. Yet this kinship also had a limiting side. Musicians are mostly dreamers, and dreamers spending time with other dreamers often means that reality rarely comes into the picture. And relationships built on just dreams often evaporate in a hurry.

George Morgan understood dreams and dreamers, but he had also once observed that Nashville's best and strongest marriages were the unions between couples where only one of the mates was in the music business. A host of others in Music City agreed with this rule—musical marriages usually produce sour notes. Yet that didn't keep Lorrie from falling in love with one of George Jones's band members, Ron Gaddis. And at an age where many girls were buying dresses for college formals, she was looking for a wedding gown. Unfortunately, the old Opry axiom was correct this time, Lorrie's first marriage had been about as much success as her recording career had experienced to date. The union lasted but a year. Yet even though the dream had quickly shattered, the marriage hadn't left Lorrie completely void of anything of worth. The young woman had been blessed with a beautiful little girl, Morgan.

Single motherhood for a woman just twenty-one who was trying to carve out a music career was going to be

tough. Many would have simply given up one or the
other. Yet Lorrie loved her daughter even more than she
loved the business. She had had good role models as
parents, and she knew that the family came before anything. And with her mother stepping in to help, she also
knew that just like her father, she could still make the
music work too. She would just have to scale back and
be patient. Certainly patience was something that she had
been taught firsthand through the experience of the past
four years.

More than ever, as she spent time being a mother, she
turned to songwriting. And though young for that field,
Lorrie was dedicated. "When I'm alone with my music,"
she explained in almost every interview she gave, "I can
listen a little closer to what it's all about.

"I use that time alone singing and writing to keep my
voice in shape, to really focus on my style, but most
importantly, just to keep a close personal rapport with
my music. You have to have your heart in your music to
make it more meaningful and enjoyable for the audience."

That audience was now mainly centered around Nashville as Lorrie was performing in places like George
Jones's club, Possum Holler, as well as Jerry Reed's
Country Place. She was gaining a bit of exposure and
her natural way of working the crowd was beginning to
turn some of Music City's most skeptical heads, but no
one was offering any deals. In spite of having folks say
that she was good, she apparently wasn't good enough
to earn a solid deal with a company that had the money
to really promote her.

In 1981, when a young redhead named Reba was beginning to jump up the ladder of success and Barbara
Mandrell and her sisters, Louise and Irlene, were the hottest stars on television, Lorrie was back performing for
the Opry fans and opening for the likes of Billy Thunderkloud, Jack Greene, and Jeannie Seely.

Jack Greene and Jeannie Seely had known Lorrie for
years. Both were long-time members of the Opry and had
watched her grow up. They could talk about the way she

had charmed the audience on her debut. They could tell stories about her father George, too. Yet Jeannie hadn't been in the top ten since 1973 when she had hit number six with "Can I Sleep in Your Arms?" The peak of her popularity had been in the late sixties.

Greene, who had begun his climb to solo success as a member of Ernest Tubb's band, hadn't been in the top ten since 1969. His last number one had been "Statue of a Fool," and that had been over a decade before. Like Seely, on the road he drew a crowd that a decade later would be hitting the road and heading to Branson. Neither of these acts had much of a following with the crowd who were buying Waylon, Willie, Barbara, Ronnie, and Eddie.

Billy Thunderkloud was a Canadian Native American who had once headed up the Chieftones. Mainly known for appearing in Indian costumes, the artist charted only a few times in the mid-seventies. In most circles, Lorrie was better known than Billy.

Such was Morgan's lot. She needed exposure to get a deal, but she wasn't landing gigs that exposed her talents to the right crowds. She needed the young audience to interest a record label, but to actively seek those crowds meant having to turn her back on the Opry. She wanted to become an official member of the Opry and perform there each week with her old friends, yet without a hit record she wasn't going to be invited. No matter where she looked, there always seemed to be a "Catch 22" situation.

Now that she had a daughter to support, logic should have told the twenty-two-year-old to hang it up. The deck was stacked against her. She might have had the talent, but she just didn't have the financial resources and the time to battle this new wave of stars. Besides, she was loyal to the old Nashville, the one where her father and his friends had been the stars. The new Nashville was changing and it wasn't a change that Lorrie seemed to appreciate. The Opry was no longer at the heart of the most popular performers' lives. Deep down, Lorrie knew that if being a star meant giving up on her Opry dream, she wasn't going to do it. Yet everyone in the business now believed that a performer couldn't have both anymore.

Chapter 4

As the eighties made way for the explosion of the country band sound and more and more young adults got onto the country music bandwagon, Lorrie Morgan needed something that would jumpstart her solo career. Alabama had dramatically changed the country music landscape and because of this change, Lorrie was literally stuck in the water without a paddle, and she was going to need some help fighting her way upstream. Few at the time would have guessed that the struggling single mother would have gotten that from her ex-husband Ron Gaddis. Yet it was this chance from her former spouse that gave her the break that began her slow climb back up Music City's success ladder.

Not long after they had divorced, Lorrie received a tip from Ron that his old boss George Jones was looking for a female duet partner to use on his road shows. With George and Tammy having broken up again, Jones had a long list of duet hits that didn't make much sense without a woman singing along. In other words, he had a huge hole in his live show he had to fill. It didn't take much begging by Ron until Lorrie had called and made plans for the audition.

Ms. Morgan had long been a fan of Ms. Wynette's songs, and like most inside the music business, had also long admired George Jones's unique contribution to Nashville's honky-tonk sound. Yet never in her wildest dreams had Lorrie ever planned on stepping into Tammy's shoes onstage. Now that she had the chance, she wondered if the unpredictable Jones would think she measured up to the standards created by his ex-wife, the ''Queen of Country Heartache.''

As she would soon find out, Lorrie wasn't alone in seeking this break. Several other local female talents lined up to audition for the spot on the Jones's bill. Some of these Tammy-wannabes had a great resumé, a solid voice, and knew George's material well. A few of them looked as if they could step right in. And it was well-known that Jones wanted to make this transition as easy as he could on himself and his band. Rumor had it that three or four of these women were being seriously considered for the part until the beautiful Morgan waltzed into the room. George had admired Lorrie's father and his music, he loved the way Lorrie carried herself, and when he heard her sing "Golden Rings," he was immediately convinced that he had found just the right opening act and duet partner. Auditions were shut down and old George left to celebrate his discovery.

For Lorrie this new gig should have signaled a real shot at impressing not only the powers that be at the major record labels, but also the millions of George Jones fans across the nation. George, an important part of the music business for two decades, was coming off the best two years of his life. He had hit the top with "Still Doing Time," and "He Stopped Loving Her Today." The latter won the CMA's Single of the Year award. Jones had also taken home the honor of CMA's Male Vocalist of the Year two years running. Everyone seemed to want a piece of George. Even straight arrows like Barbara Mandrell were telling the world that they were huge Jones fans and wanted to get him in the studio to record with them.

Yet while George's career was riding high, his personal life was sinking fast. His well-publicized bouts with alcohol and drugs had left some wondering if he wasn't about to self-destruct. His break-up with Tammy Wynette had seen him taking more than a few low blows from the press. The rumor that he was extremely unhappy and depressed had many friends concerned about his health. Yet in the face of all of this, his bookers still put him out on the road in front of the public for more than 200 days a year. Because of the old edict of "making hay

while the sun shone,'' George and his band were working
like dogs: A number of Morgan's friends warned her that
this kind of life was like nothing the young mother and
singer had ever experienced. Yet nothing that anyone said
could have prepared Lorrie for what she about to experience on her ''grand tour.''

It didn't take Lorrie Morgan long to begin to understand why so much of the country music world loved this
man. When he sang onstage, she would say that it made
chills run up her spine. And the fans just didn't listen to
him, they responded to him. Even more than that they
seemed to worship the ground on which he walked. Even
though he often didn't even acknowledge them after the
show, they stayed and begged to meet him. He was their
hero, their idol, and on the best nights he held them in a
trance from the moment he walked on stage until the
second he left. His fans couldn't get enough of him. And
that was the upside, because there were times the fans
paid for a ticket and got none of him.

The master showman had a habit of not showing up
on time. And when he did, sometimes all hell would
break loose. His moods shifted suddenly. He sometimes
just appeared not to care about anything. There were
times when he seemed to want to antagonize the crowd.
Some had called him an impossible act to follow, but
sometimes the same could be said about trying to work
with him.

Lorrie would go out first and perform her set. She was
the opener and was supposed to set the mode for the rest
of the show. The length of Lorrie's set would often depend upon if one of the band members had been able to
find George. At times they would find him, bring him to
the stage, and things would go fine. At other times he
would be drunk by the time they tracked him down and
the resulting show would reflect Jones's state. He would
forget words, miss cues, even walk off stage and leave
the venue without warning. And when things like this
happened the crowd would sometimes grow very ugly.

Yet the nights when George was drunk were much
better than those when he simply wouldn't show up at

all. On those evenings, Lorrie would sing every song she knew, stall as long as she could, and then announce that Jones was sick and was unable to perform. The patrons, who had paid a high dollar to see their idol, usually knew what had caused the "illness" and would often launch things at the stage. With Lorrie and the band as targets, the fans would vent their frustrations. It was often scary and would sometimes turn into a near riot. On more than one occasion, Lorrie actually feared for her life.

She later told William Kerns of the *Avalanche-Journal* in Lubbock, Texas, "At the age of 21, I couldn't handle it very well. In fact, it was pretty frightening. There would be people throwing things at you whenever George didn't show up for a show. And there were times when we had to lie down on the floor of the bus because the people were so mad about George not being there, they would actually rock the bus."

In 1990 Lorrie shed a bit more light on George's dark side and her dark two years with him when she told Steve Metsch of the *Decatur (Illinois) Herald & Review,* "George Jones is a great singer and a legend, but during the time I worked with him, he had a lot of problems with drugs and alcohol."

Yet Lorrie stuck it out, keeping quiet about Jones's problems and supporting him to the press and the public. When her friends wondered why she didn't quit, she couldn't fully explain to them just how good George was when he was sober. She also couldn't explain what it was like to sing with him when everything was right. At times all the hell seemed worth it for the few bits of heaven that made the road something special.

Yet looking back from more than a decade down that long road, Lorrie realized the full toll that working with Jones had taken on her life. He worked everyday, night after night and never seemed to rest. She later admitted it was something that she was glad she did, because it taught her a lot about the business, but she also quickly admitted that she would never want to work that hard again. Nor would she want to face that kind of unpredictable behavior either.

It took two years for Lorrie to come to grips with the fact that the bad times with George far outweighed the good. When she finally admitted that she couldn't take the pressure of one-night stands and never knowing what kind of condition George would show up in, Morgan not only left the Jones show, but almost left the music business all together. The pressure and the lifestyle just didn't seem worth it to her. In order to get a grip on life, she moved back in with her mother and looked for something local. If she was going to stay in the music business, she didn't want to have to leave her little girl or go through regular trips to the "Twilight Zone."

In hindsight, it would be easy to speculate on why Lorrie even considered giving music another shot. George Jones had showed her not only the dynamic highs, but the extreme lows too. And if the experience with Jones had been her only one in the business, then she probably would have chosen to walk away. Yet before she had travelled with Jones, Lorrie had watched another famous George handle this business and the fans much better. She had witnessed firsthand how shows could be run and how fans could be treated. If anything kept pulling her back to seeking out another chance in Music City, it had to be the example she had seen in George Morgan's life.

Lorrie didn't have to look very long to find a job. In the midst of the country music boom, she discovered a local theme park looking for talent.

"I heard that they were doing auditions in the park (Opryland)," Lorrie recalled in a 1991 press release, "and I decided to try out. I was so nervous I couldn't get to sleep, so I stayed up drinking coffee and practicing, and by the time I got there, I was hoarse and shaking from all that caffeine, and I totally bombed. It was a joke. I thought I'd blown it, but Bob Whitaker, who was head of entertainment at the park, had heard me sing on the Opry, and he knew I could do it. So he took me off to the side and said, 'Why don't you come back tomorrow and try this again?' I came back the next day and got a job."

Whitaker put Lorrie in a bluegrass show. Not only had Morgan never sung bluegrass, but she didn't even like bluegrass! Even though she had an initial bad feeling about performing a type of music that she didn't care for, Lorrie went to rehearsal, and within weeks was doing seven or eight bluegrass shows a day.

This Opryland gig included some other performers who would go on to stardom. Some of the men and women who shared the stage with Lorrie included fiddler Mack Magaha (from the Porter Waggoner show) and Dean Dillon (now a well-respected songwriter). Dillon even pitched Lorrie one of his songs, "Miami, My Amy." Morgan liked it, but with no record deal didn't feel that she could do much with it, so she let it pass. As it turned out, the song would come back to her in a special way a few years down the road.

Opryland was a good clean way to make a living. There were few angry fans and no drunks. It was a venue filled with good, clean family fun. It was a welcome change of pace after two years on the road with Jones. Yet the job in the bluegrass show didn't offer many opportunities for upward movement. Most of the folks who worked with Morgan knew that they were never going to be spotlighted big-time entertainers. The show simply offered an opportunity at some regular money. While that was fine for most, Lorrie wanted more. She still had big dreams and she had the drive to want to see a few of those dreams come true. This show was therefore just a stopgap.

While Lorrie was working her stint in the Opryland Theme Park at the Country Bluegrass Show, another old friend called and offered her another bone. It wasn't big time and it wasn't a record deal, but it was a chance at more local exposure. Ralph Emery wanted to use Lorrie as a regular vocalist on his local morning television show. This WSM offering was a version of the same show which had once featured Morgan's father from time to time and had given Lorrie her first shot at singing on television when she was a small child. Lorrie jumped at the chance. Much more than the bluegrass show, Ralph's program would give her a real opportunity to remind many of the local movers and shakers that she was still an untapped talent.

"I've know Ralph since I was five," she told members of the press when remembering the chance he had given her at the very time when her career had seemed to be on its last legs. "Ralph and Dad were good friends. Ralph was like a second dad to me, because he would get on to me when he thought I was doing wrong, and he was very quick to tell me his opinion, which I respected a lot and still do. It was a great situation for me."

It was highly doubtful that working on local television or at the park would have meant much to Lorrie's career. These outlets gave her a chance to perform, kept her in the business and paid some bills, but they just didn't offer much in the way of advancement. Not that many of the Music City decisionmakers took much note of what she was doing. What Lorrie couldn't have guessed was that the very folks who had given her these seemingly insignificant breaks, would give her a plum that would turn her career around by introducing her to millions who had never even heard her name. Soon, Lorrie would find herself being beamed prime-time into living rooms around America on a nightly basis.

When the owners of Opryland announced that with the growth of cable television and the success of country music on the networks, they were going to launch a cable network of their own, it really changed the face of country music. Once thought of as local or regional, the genre now had a national forum on which to build. One of the linchpins of this network would be a nightly entertainment/talk show anchored by long-time Nashville disc jockey and personality, Ralph Emery. As was soon to become obvious, TNN couldn't have made a wiser opening move.

Emery decided that the format that had worked so well on WSM in the morning would also do well on a national level in the evening. So he took a great deal of that show's talent and production staff with him when he moved his operations to the new studio at the Opryland

Theme Park. To her delight, Lorrie made the trip with Ralph and the morning show's other regulars, Tom Brant and Darlene Austin, to cableland. Even though she didn't realize it at the time, landing a gig as a regular on *Nashville Now* would prove to be a very big deal. After years of working one-night stands, small clubs, and shows at theme parks, this would prove to be her most important break to date. Yet in many ways what got her the exposure she needed to save her career at the time, also might have held her back a bit too.

A decade later Morgan explained to *Country Fever* how working on TNN had at first worked against her. "I was on Ralph's show from the time it began and people in the industry didn't take me seriously as an artist because they had the attitude that 'Oh, she's just that local girl' and they were on the lookout for the next new artist to come from the outside."

At about the same time that Lorrie realized that she was being overlooked time and time again, Pam Tillis was also scolding Nashville for looking outside the city for new talent. It seemed that artists who grew up in town, as well as artists who had famous names, simply weren't given many breaks by those who controlled the record labels. Many thought nothing fresh could be found at home. In doing so, they were overlooking not only an immense stash of talent, but what should have been obvious—with the advent of TNN there was a huge retail market for country music that wasn't solely dependent on radio. Overnight country music had brand-new buyers ready and willing sitting out in Middle America waiting for new product!

Lorrie sensed, correctly too, that this new TNN audience would have bought her product if she had one. Yet for years the people who were tuned into Ralph's *Nashville Now* were largely overlooked· by the majority of those selling product to retailers. These weren't the young, new country fans, they were the old fans of the past. These people had disposable income, but Music City wasn't offering the product that they wanted to spend it on. TNN had tapped into the market, and that market loved Lorrie, but the folks in town couldn't seem to understand how to translate that into dollars at the retail outlet. Eventually when Nashville failed to capitalize on this large market base, Branson, Missouri did. And it meant millions for the Ozarks too!

This lack of respect from the record labels was frustrating to people like Lorrie Morgan and Pam Tillis, but the fact that she was a regular on cable's most successful new show figured to get Lorrie a second look in another arena in which she so desperately wanted to secure a spot. With the solid ratings numbers in hand, and the fact that the folks who loved her on *Nashville Now* were also the bread and butter of the Opry crowds, Lorrie felt that she finally had earned a shot at a regular Saturday night spot to go with her Monday through Friday cable gig. After all, in another era, hadn't her father's huge drawing card with the radio audience in Wheeling gotten him his Opry invitation? This seemed to be the same thing.

With her *Nashville Now* success, Lorrie began in earnest to lobby the Opry manager Hal Durham about securing a spot on the show. The fact that she was offering her services was not news to Durham. She had been bugging Hal for seven years, and it had created a huge dilemma for him. In truth he would have loved to have invited Lorrie to join, but he couldn't get past the fact that she didn't have a hit record. If she could just get some kind a moderate hit, then he could open the door a bit. Even though he regretted it, Hal had to explain that television didn't write her membership invitation, only radio and record success did that. In other words, the rules were still the same as they always had been even though the game had changed dramatically. She seemed so ready for what she wanted most, and yet she couldn't get in because of some seemingly outdated rules. For a young woman who had once made history at the Opry, this thinking made it all the more frustrating.

Yet even though it may have not been obvious to the Opry, in a sense Lorrie had come a long way in a relatively short period of time and was on the cutting edge of a country music revolution. Lorrie had learned a great deal on her journey, too! If she had taken a quick inventory she could have counted several important milestones that had fallen in her favor. She had survived two years with George Jones and in the face of personal threats on her life by some of his angry fans, she had determined that she still wanted to continue in the business. In spite of the fallout of having to admit that she had messed up her first attempt at marriage, Morgan had also discovered her own ability to love unconditionally through her daughter. She had grown closer to her mother as the two of them had sought out ways to make Lorrie's personal and public choices work. She had taken a job just to make ends meet, be close to her daughter, and stay in touch with the business, and that job had led to her expanding her range and her musical outlook. And finally, she had discovered that old friends never forget you and will always be there to give you a break when they can.

Two years before, Lorrie had been going nowhere. Now, she was at least someone whose name and voice were known and appreciated by millions of country music fans. While she wasn't ruling the charts and network television like Barbara Mandrell, and even if she wasn't about ready to hit passing gear and race up the charts like Reba McEntire, she was moving forward and in sight of the big time. So for the time being, Lorrie had to be satisfied in having a pretty good foundation on which to build a career.

Chapter 5

What Lorrie lacked to give her a shot at the big time and a chance to finally live her dreams by becoming an Opry member was a record deal. She didn't lack that deal because of lack of effort. She was knocking on doors, hoping and praying that a lot of movers and shakers were catching her on *Nashville Now*, and calling all the folks of influence she still knew to see if they could help her get a deal. Yet even with all the work she had done and all the personal progress she had made, she was still wondering if anyone would see her potential and offer her a chance to record again for a label. In late 1983, four years after she last placed a song on the charts, a voice from the past called her in to negotiate a contract. Finally she was going to have a shot at recording again.

MCA, the folks who had contacted Lorrie, was a hot label. Among others, their stable included the country's hottest female act, Barbara Mandrell. But Mandrell, whose successful NBC television show had earned her the title of the ''Sweetheart of Saturday Night,'' was just the beginning of their long list of hitmakers. MCA had also recently signed Reba McEntire away from Mercury. They seemed to be working on cornering the market on Nashville's hottest females. With that in mind and sensing that Lorrie might just be seasoned enough to join Mandrell and McEntire on radio playlists, the label cut a deal with Morgan.

It was almost an understatement to say that Lorrie seemed excited about landing her newest record gig. She knew that second chances were rare in Music City and this one was to be treasured. Yet she was also smart enough to realize that the label wasn't going to give her much time to reach her potential. The business had changed and under the new rules, an artist wasn't given very long to earn success and praise. She was going to have to hit fast and move quickly.

While keeping her fingers crossed and lighting a few candles, Lorrie told all those around her that this MCA deal was a good one. "We've got all the parts in place this time. The formula fits," she said. Yet many didn't believe that MCA really would take Lorrie as seriously as they did Reba. It seemed that if Morgan was going to make it, it would have to initially be on her own.

Lorrie at least publicly stated that the producers which MCA had assigned her, Ronnie Gant and Jim Vinneau, were the right ones for the job. She also revealed that the label had promised that when her product was released that they would have great promotion to back it up. Still acting somewhat more reserved than most women who had just been signed by a major label, Lorrie told her fans and the press that "we have a chance (now) to go for the gold." Even in the euphoria created in her camp by the new deal, Lorrie knew that there were no guarantees.

Lorrie's past highest chart climb had stopped at number seventy-five. MCA felt that Ralph Emery's audience would help push her first record release of 1984 higher than that. The company quickly discovered that they had figured wrong. "Don't Go Changing," which had been a pop release for Billy Joel, had been shipped in March. It had found the charts soon thereafter, but was mysteriously not around in late April. Shocking many, the release peaked at number sixty-nine and spent just five weeks on the playlists. This is the face of *Billboard* having recommended the single to its stations with the comments, "A low-key devotional that highlights Morgan's bright, firm vocals." The recommendation did little to impress the radio stations' programming directors. In truth there was no way around it, the single bombed. "Don't Go Changing" hadn't changed Morgan's performance record.

A major part of MCA's problem may have been the

fact that the label really didn't know who Lorrie was. They seemed to think of her in terms usually reserved for a beauty queen, playmate, or movie sex symbol. The talent that was so obvious to those who watched her work each week on *Nashville Now* seemed lost on those in public relations. They weren't highlighting her voice as much as they were her body. And by pushing her as a sex kitten more than an entertainer, MCA was not only missing so much of what Lorrie really was, but who her audience was too.

On stage Lorrie was not just another up-and-coming act. She was something special. Morgan was a pro who could still charm a crowd like she had that first night at the Opry. Yet now she had the confidence to know that she had a gift. While walking in the spotlight, the usually shy and reserved Lorrie had catlike reflexes and wonderful enthusiasm. Night after night she would rip the heck out of Jerry Lee Lewis's "Great Balls of Fire," and shake the roof with Creedance Clearwater Revival's "Bad Moon Rising." The crowds who turned out to catch her act, also loved her when she did a few of her own tunes and embraced the sound of her father through her rendition of "Candy Kisses." How could MCA not have seen this power and harnessed it in the studio was a mystery to almost everyone who observed Morgan in person or on television. It was almost as if the label had never talked to her, watched her work, or looked at her background. The only thing those writing her press releases consistently seemed to notice was her "curves." Looking at her bio, it would have made more sense for her to have been selling an exercise and beauty video tape.

Yet even though MCA was largely in the dark as to what to do with her, one very powerful entertainer who was also known for her "curves" took note of Lorrie's real potential and talent and jumped in to take advantage of what she saw. Even though it would take a few weeks for word to get to Lorrie, one of her long-time idols and role models had decided to try to make something happen for George Morgan's youngest daughter. What transpired next seemed almost too good to be true.

When Sandy Gallin first tried to reach her, Lorrie didn't return the call. She didn't know who Sandy Gallin was and the message he had left gave no hint as to what Mr. Gallin wanted. Not giving up easily, Gallin touched base with MCA Nashville and informed the company that he was interested in one of their acts. MCA then tracked Lorrie down and informed the singer that Sandy, the man who wanted to visit with her, was the powerful West Coast manager of another blond country music entertainer, Dolly Parton. Best of all, he was interested in working with Lorrie too. At that point Lorrie decided to return his call.

Morgan soon discovered that Dolly wasn't Gallin's only client. The powerful entertainment executive from Katz-Gallin-Morey Enterprises also handled Mac Davis, Joan Rivers, Sally Struthers, Richard Simmons, and Beverly D'Angelo. As Morgan visited with Gallin, she discovered that it had been Dolly herself who had recommended to Sandy that he immediately sign Lorrie. Ms. Parton had caught Lorrie on *Nashville Now* and thought she had star quality. After Gallin watched a few tapes and listened to some demos, he readily agreed that Dolly knew what she was talking about. Upon meeting Morgan on the phone, Sandy invited her to come see him in Los Angeles and work out details for representation.

From their first meeting, Gallin sensed that the young woman with a lifetime of experience under her belt, was a superstar in the raw. Even though she hadn't produced any hits or was even a well-known commodity outside of the Opry house and the *Nashville Now* audience, she carried herself with the confidence of someone who had that quality that spoke "stardom." Not wanting to waste any time, Sandy signed Lorrie as quickly as he could, touched base with MCA, and then immediately began to plug her to all of the influential sources he knew in New York, Los Angeles, and Music City. Practically overnight the news of the signing was making entertainment trades everywhere, and thousands of writers, critics, and bookers were trying to get more information on the woman who Dolly predicted was going to be a big star.

With Morgan now seemingly all over the entertainment map, and in spite of the fact that her first record had not captured magic and scored big numbers, everything should have been right with the world. After all, who wouldn't have wanted to have been picked for stardom by the powerful L.A.-based management firm? Yet what most experts thought Gallin had planned for Lorrie worried many of the singer's friends and boosters in Nashville. Some believed that Gallin's master plan included using what Lorrie had built in the way of a country base to spin her over to the pop charts. Maybe even make her over into a Hollywood movie star. Her friends wanted Lorrie to be successful, but they didn't want George Morgan's girl to desert town and leave behind the music that had made her father famous.

While rumors were running wild, most everyone's fears were purely speculative as no one in Nashville seemed to really know what Sandy had in mind for his big Morgan push. Even Lorrie seemed unsure of what would be going on in the future. She told writer Jack Hurst, "We know we want to have me have strong country roots. That's what I feel, and that's what I sing more than anything. Basically, the plan is to try to keep it country for a while and then eventually probably cross over somewhere down the line."

Yet even as Lorrie spoke about pop possibilities, she seemed to hang onto her country roots with a firm hand. While she admitted liking Michael Jackson and Boy George, her role models were not them nor the pop/country female stars of the day. Barbara Mandrell, Dolly Parton, and Crystal Gayle were great, but in Lorrie's mind they almost always took a back seat to Connie Smith, Tammy Wynette, and Jean Shepard. These were the women she had watched from the wings of the Opry as a child. She freely admitted that she loved their style more than anyone who had come out in the last decade. These were the women she wanted to emulate, and not one of them had gone pop. Most of them had even hung onto their big hair and were proud to appear on *Hee Haw*. Besides, hadn't Tanya Tucker just proven that country acts didn't play well in rock and that Music City radio outlets quit playing them when they tried? So deep down, Lorrie must have figured that even a California P.R. firm wasn't going to change her a lot. Her blood was filled with too much twang to ever squeeze it all out. So beyond signing Lorrie, the industry's biggest question was what was Sandy Gallin going to do with her?

Initially the news of the signing appeared to pay off even if no one knew the direction Morgan's new firm wanted to go. Lorrie used her strong new management team, as well as her *Now* shots and her MCA deal, to gain a nomination for the Academy of Country Music's "Most Promising Female Vocalist Award." Few, if any, thought that Lorrie had a chance to win the award, after all, she had only spent sixteen total weeks on the Billboard charts in the past five years, but many believed that this forum would at the least allow country music's new hip audience to finally meet the new MCA artist and see Morgan's potential.

Lorrie lost as expected. Gus Hardin walked away with the win in the "Most Promising" category at the West Coast-based show. But after years of working far away from the national scene, this exposure on network television was a big plus for Morgan too. Ironically, Hardin may have grabbed the award from Lorrie and three others, but she really never came close to fulfilling her promise. She would never hit the top ten with a solo record after this night. Within two years RCA would drop Gus Hardin as a recording artist.

As Lorrie began to take advantage of her new exposure by leaving home and hitting the road to play more dates in front of live audiences, back in Nashville something special was going on behind the scenes at the place that Lorrie had always considered her first home. Hal Durham was beginning to wrangle Morgan an invitation to join the big show.

To Lorrie, the Opry had always almost seemed like a church. It was a place where people came to be renewed, as well as to rediscover themselves, their goals, and their music. Like a house of worship, it was almost hallowed. Every performance there was important, none could be blown off. This was the place to come and celebrate, mourn, and to learn. This was not a place of big bucks, but of big hearts. And there were more big people here than big stars. To an honored few this special stage was home. In Morgan's mind no one ever got too big for the Opry and no award could ever mean as much as being accepted into this exclusive club.

"I had been around the Opry since I was a baby," she explained. "And I've done numerous guest appearances. If someone had to cancel, they'd call me to fill in quite a bit. When dad passed away when I was sixteen, I went to Hal Durham and said, 'I want to be a member!' He said, 'It's not time yet.' For a long time I called every week and asked, 'Do you need me to go on?' Sometimes they would, but a lot of times it was, 'No, not this week.' After the awards show, though, they signed me as a member." It was finally time.

Lorrie's getting the ACM award nomination had given Hal the ammunition he needed to push her through the invitation process. Even if Lorrie didn't have a hit record, she now had the look of a real star. For the first time, the Opry could justify that it wasn't inviting her simply because she was one of the show's most popular member's kids. She was being invited because she was worthy of the honor and because she had proven that she would not take this honor lightly.

In a sense, Lorrie came back to the womb in 1984 simply by joining the Grand Ole Opry. This was where her career had really been born. This was where her father's memory still lived. Many even said how appropriate it was to have the child of the man who had sung the last song at the old Opry house, to join the cast at the new one. Yet even though Hal had pushed her through and scores were thrilled, Lorrie's invitation was not without some controversy.

A few Opry members didn't want Lorrie because she hadn't had a hit record and they felt that she hadn't paid enough dues. Though the lovely girl was a favorite with the crowd, some performers were also seeing Ms. Morgan in the same way they perceived Ernest Tubb's son, Justin—a second generation novelty act. Yet how the fans and some of the brass saw her didn't bother Lorrie. She would tell Joe Edwards of the Associated Press, "Singing on the Opry is like a dream come true. It's a way to carry on my dad's name." And that was something she had long ago vowed to do. How proud George would have been too!

Lorrie's all-important induction date was Saturday, June 9. Joining her on that night's bill were Stonewall Jackson, Connie Smith, Dell Reeves, Jeannie Seely, Jim Ed Brown, Bill Anderson, Jean Shepard, Roy Acuff, Dottie West, Jan Howard, and a host of other regulars. So even though "today's big stars" were someplace else, it was a fan fest weekend that presented a very special moment for country music's real fans to celebrate. Lorrie Morgan became the youngest Opry member ever.

"Justin Tubb and I are the only two members of the Opry who were signed without a hit record (actually George Morgan hadn't had one either)," Lorrie would proudly explain to those who asked why this honor that had been so quickly passed over by today's hottest stars was so important to her. Morgan added, "It was because of our dedication to the Opry (that we were signed). Hal knew I love the Opry and that I was dedicated to it." And dedicated she was. So much so that it wasn't long before the people at MCA, as well as Sandy Gallin, were concerned. They wondered if tying herself to this "old horse" would also stall her move on the charts and country music radio. After all, the Opry didn't drive playlists anymore. The old stage had long ago become a place to sing old hits, not make new ones.

After appearing on the Opry as a member, Lorrie really got going on her career. She formed her own band called Something Special, and then began to put together concert dates. Yet to really make a complete package, she needed a booker. Within weeks of her acceptance as an

Opry member, she had joined one of the town's best firms.

On July 16, 1984, Top Billing International announced that they would be handling all of Lorrie's future bookings. "We are tremendously excited over the prospect of representing such a beautiful and talented person," said Top Billing's chairman of the board Tandy Rice.

Lorrie was excited too. She echoed something she had said when she had been signed by MCA, "We've got all the parts in place at this time." What that meant was that she thought she was about to really take off. A lot of people were predicting she would too!

Joining the Opry, landing the recording contract, and signing with a big agency, as well as catching on with one of the industry's best bookers, were solid breaks. But the real place where Lorrie was mainly getting noted was still *Nashville Now*. The beautiful and gifted singer was one of the most eagerly anticipated parts of the show. When she wasn't there to sing for them, scores in the live audience and tens of thousands at home were disappointed. That popularity meant something too! A year after its debut, the Ralph Emery–hosted show was reaching over twelve million homes, and many of the viewers were latching onto Lorrie as one of their own. She was getting sacks of mail each week. Her fan club was growing by leaps and bounds. It seemed as she had finally crossed the desert of bad breaks and was ready to take part in the big time. Yet it wasn't destined to be that easy. It seemed that as quickly as things came together, they also started to fall apart.

Lorrie's relationship with Gallin was beginning to show signs of strain. Sandy's company partnership split up, forcing the L.A.-based consultant to reorganize. During this period, Lorrie was placed on the back burner. Morgan knew she didn't have much time to cool her heels. She needed results now. MCA wanted a hit, and if she had to wait for Sandy to blow her horn, she might not have a record deal to trumpet. So she parted ways with Gallin. Few noticed any falloff that could be traced to leaving the West Coast firm.

As the year wound down and Morgan finished what had been a very busy schedule of appearances, Lorrie joined television stars Todd Bridges and Ed Begley Jr. for the 28th Annual Telethon of Stars for Easter Seals in St. Louis. Seen in four states, this much-watched media event not only raised money for a good cause, but raised a sense of awareness of Lorrie on the budding country music prospect. Yet even as she was introduced as a recording artist, her status with her record label was in doubt.

By mid-year MCA had been reviewing her contract and her potential and were thinking about cutting her loose. Even though no one would mention it at the time, the record label hadn't wanted Lorrie to join the Opry. Logic told them that Alabama's fans didn't care a thing about the Opry. Most of the new patrons of country music thought that being a part of the Opry show meant you were not cool. The label actually thought that Lorrie being a part of country music's most hallowed show created an image that would be too hard to market. They didn't seem to want her to be real country, they just wanted her to use country to appeal to crossover fans. Ultimately it seemed that MCA just couldn't figure out how to market an act that they believed wouldn't get in step with the times.

Just a few months before Lorrie's career had appeared so promising, now it seemed to be headed in the wrong direction. Everyone of the new movers and shakers was convinced that the only way for Lorrie to make it as a star, was to desert the very traditions and ties that had made her love country music in the beginning. If giving up her loyalty and lying about who she was was the formula for success in the eighties, then Morgan didn't need success. And even if the label deserted her and Lorrie couldn't turn the backward momentum around, and even if she never topped the playlists or cut another single, she at least had managed to use her MCA deal to capture her most important dream. She was a member of the Opry and that was something that had nothing to do with public relations or record deals. In her case it had to do with character, and George Morgan had always figured that if you didn't have character, you didn't have anything. He had taught this lesson to his daughter well too. In 1984 she might have given up her chance at the big time, but she had finally come home. And being home felt good even when things were going bad.

Chapter 6

MCA wanted to sell Lorrie as a sophisticated singer. The label seemed to believe that a little country edge was fine, just so it was subdued. This trying to take the country out of the performer was not a new tack in the record industry. Back in the fifties, Elvis had been groomed to fit in with the city folks. So had Jim Reeves. So while Porter Waggoner and Roy Acuff may have missed their appointments, these makeovers were not all together unusual.

For Morgan and other female artists, the label looked at folks like Barbara Mandrell as role models. She was the complete package. In Morgan they saw a young woman who already could look at home on both the streets of New York and Los Angeles. And that was great! What they didn't seem to want to see was a woman who fit in on the stage of the Opry. More importantly, they really didn't seem to want this singer being remembered as an actual member of the Opry. And they certainly didn't want anyone to look at Morgan and think back to the glory days of Connie Smith or Loretta Lynn or the ''sophistication'' of clogging. Old was out and new, fresh, crossover youth-oriented country was in. MCA wanted Lorrie to reflect that new image.

This was hardly new thinking. Dating back more than two decades, record labels in Nashville had constantly been trying to take the hick out of their female artists. In the past these transformations had been performed on the likes of Lynn Anderson, Tammy Wynette, and even to a certain degree Barbara Mandrell. Recently Music City had transformed Reba McEntire from a barrel-racing-tomboy-grocery-shopping-coupon-clipping rural wife into a sexy, sensational Fifth Avenue department store glamour queen. Now they thought it was time to work with Lorrie, but in this case, the makeover would be more mental than physical. It would be more about taste, choice, and substance, and less about style.

In truth this project appeared to be easy. MCA had been forced to bring Reba a lot further than they ever were going to have to bring Lorrie. After all, the singer already had the glamour. Her beauty would have worked in Hollywood as well as Broadway, and she had always dressed in modern, sophisticated ensembles. Even the least observant person could quickly see that Morgan had the classy look down already. So what the label wanted to change didn't concern what she wore, it concerned the crowd she ran with.

MCA wanted Morgan to separate herself from the Opry. The label believed that this membership made her seem too old-fashioned. They felt that for Morgan to be a hip act, one who rubbed elbows with movie stars and pop singers, she was going to have dump undesirables like Minnie Pearl and Bill Anderson. Many saw this as something as simple as a phone call and then—presto—a bunch of Saturday nights were free. Of course Lorrie wouldn't see it that way.

Sometime later, after Lorrie and the label had parted ways, she would tell the press that MCA was always after her to go to certain events, be seen with certain people, and act a certain way. What the label didn't understand was that while Lorrie would work with them on studio choices, she was not going be told what to do, how to act, or who her friends could be. She also let it be known that she didn't like the social scene and didn't want to attend a function just so she could have her picture made there. She had politely complained to the record company executives that this was asking too much because, in her words, "I don't like going to clubs, I'm not a drinker and I am not a partier." MCA seemed to think she should change that philosophy.

The label didn't seem to consider the fact that Lorrie was a single mother who felt that being with her daughter

was the most important thing in life. If it meant giving
up time with Morgan, then Lorrie was not going to go
to a cocktail party for a booking agent. Her child was
also too important to sacrifice their special time together
for the sake of meaningless interviews or hours of meeting radio disc jockeys who cared more about the brand
of scotch at the complimentary bar than they did about
which artist had shown up at the party. So when the label
asked her to do something she thought was worthless,
Lorrie would usually say no. Few newly signed acts in
town were ever this assertive.

MCA and others in Nashville took this independent
attitude as a sign that Lorrie was a bitch. They couldn't
understand why the singer wasn't playing the game the
way everyone else did. Didn't she know who she was?
Surely she was aware of the new rules that were in place
in the industry. Surely she understood that executives and
programmers were the most important people in her life.
Surely she knew that her time belonged to MCA. As she
stood up to the company and explained that she didn't
mind standing for hours meeting country music's most
important assets, its fans, but had little time for executives who simply grabbed at any chance to party, many
wondered what had gotten into her. To have listened to
some, you would have thought that this polite, shy young
woman was possessed.

In reality Lorrie wasn't a candidate for exorcism, just
a woman who believed in not giving up things which
were important to her. Yet for standing up for herself and
her beliefs—family values if you will—she began to get
the reputation of someone with whom others couldn't
work. Over time this perception would prove to be anything but true. And given time, membership in the Opry
would prove to be cool too. But at this moment, in this
climate, Lorrie wasn't simply a woman ahead of her time,
she was being called a hard-headed bitch. And this reputation wasn't doing her career much good.

In retrospect, Lorrie might have pushed harder for the
record label if they had just once proved to her that they
really believed in her talents. Any intelligent person

would have had to question what it was the MCA was selling when they talked about Morgan. The label's company bio on Lorrie actually stated, "the pretty blonde who had all the right curves in all the right places." Certainly MCA was not going to package Reba this way. They sold McEntire as a singer with a dynamic style and voice. Yet it seemed that to the label, Lorrie was largely a nicely stacked body, and MCA wanted her to dress in a way that would show that asset off to its fullest.

Lorrie was not shy about taking advantage of the fact that she had been blessed with incredible looks. Yet she was prouder of her musical knowledge, her heritage, and voice than she was her figure. She also had a sharp mind and a lot of savvy and didn't want to be presented as a bimbo. And finally, all-American classy sex appeal was fine, but Morgan wasn't going to go so far as to distance herself from the ideals, values, and expectations of the Opry and its fans. And as always, when things came back to her making decisions based on protecting her Opry membership, the label really got upset. More and more it seemed as if a divorce was in the making.

Yet even though she often felt wronged, Lorrie didn't publicly berate or question her label. When she had the time and she believed in what they were pushing, she worked as hard as any performer for them. Still she wasn't getting any return on her efforts. MCA simply wasn't doing much for her, and it showed with their lack of interest in putting out new product. Not having new material not only gave her few things to talk about in interviews and onstage, but also didn't give Tandy Rice at Top Billing much of an opportunity to build her bookings either. As always she seemed to be again trapped in a Catch 22.

When she did perform at live shows, the crowds may have been small, but the paying patrons saw Lorrie entertaining as if this was the most important show she had ever done. Unlike so many new acts, she was there on time, signing autographs, being nice to the local help, and staying with each small-town reporter as long as she could. Her fans saw her on stage as a glamorous but classy model of the modern woman (something MCA should have noted). Yet it wasn't the label that caused Lorrie to dress to the nines for each new crowd, it was some advice that she had received when she was a child. Time and time again her father had pointed out that how you appeared on stage did matter. People didn't want to see you in the spotlight in the same clothes that you would wear to K-Mart. Lorrie never forgot those words and it showed.

George had also drilled into his daughter that the fans wanted her to be honest and straightforward. They didn't want to be sold a bill of goods, they wanted to get to know you. While looking great had been easy, this opening up on stage was hard for Lorrie. Though few realized it, she was innately shy. Yet she somehow overcame this shyness for the folks who came out just to see her. With the fans, and sometimes only with the fans, she let her guard down and let them see the woman who foremost loved the Opry, her father and especially them for coming to see her.

In Nashville's inner circle the most important personal judgments that are made are based on employer-employee relationships. George Morgan had treated his band as if they were coworkers, not employees. He was their friend, not their boss. And those who worked with him, loved him. Lorrie also incorporated this into her philosophy. Her band was a family and she wanted to be there for any of them whenever they needed her. On the road, they were a family. So while those at MCA may have thought that she was a bitch, those in the all-important inner circle knew that she wasn't.

Even before the news broke on the wire, most in Nashville had expected it. With little fanfare, MCA cut ties with Lorrie without ever getting her on the charts a second time. To many it seemed as if they gave up before they even got started. The label simply pointed out that there were creative differences between their producers and the artist and they thought it was in the best interest to develop some of their other talent. So, as it turned out, an invitation to the Opry was about all that Ms. Morgan had to show for her association with MCA.

Yet if MCA only made the Opry possible, then that was a good enough reason to have signed with them. Lorrie loved the Opry, she drew strength from it, and it was a constant in a life that had been filled with so many up and down rides. With that in mind and in spite of all the ways MCA had seemingly let her down, she probably should have sent them a thank you note. She really did have one of the important things she had always wanted.

One evening when she was working on an Opry show, a young man came up to her and introduced himself. Lorrie was aware of who he was, but being shy, she didn't respond too positively to his flirting and didn't allow him to obtain her phone number. Eventually the guitar-playing singer seemed to take the hint and moved on. Little did he know that he had really impressed Lorrie and that within a few hours he would get a second chance at getting to know her.

The young musician who had been so bold as to introduce himself to Lorrie was Keith Whitley. Whitley, who like Morgan had failed time and time again as a recording artist, was in the process of being divorced by his wife Kathi. For the singer whose life would soon become intertwined with Lorrie Morgan, times were hard. Yet like Lorrie, he simply had too much talent and too much time invested to give up on his career.

Whitley had been born in the rural area of Sandy Hook, Kentucky in the mid-fifties. At the age of eight he had already sung country music on local radio shows. Just entering his teens, he and Ricky Skaggs became friends, began to sing together and caught on with country music veterans, the Stanley Brothers. Keith was just fifteen when he made his Opry debut and had cut more than a half dozen albums with the Stanleys by the time he was old enough to drive a car. After playing with several different bands during his late teens, he returned to work with the Stanley Brothers in the late seventies. It was during this period that he met and fell in love with Kathi. Their union would last six years.

In 1983 Keith moved to Nashville and a year later

landed an RCA recording contract. Things went south for a while, and Kathi grew tired of Keith's fondness for alcohol and his constant effort to revive broken dreams. Finally she could take no more and left. As he watched the woman he loved walk away, Keith had to have wondered if his more than two decades of work had been worth all the pain and heartache.

A number of Whitley's close friends told him that his main problem wasn't a lack of talent or a string of bad luck, it was his inability to control an addiction. Realizing that they were right, the struggling singer even checked into a hospital and tried to beat his problems with the bottle. One of the wonders of Keith's life was that in the face of all of his career disappointments and his problems with booze, RCA kept plugging. Lorrie Morgan had barely been given a chance by MCA before being dropped, and she had caused few problems. Across town, RCA not only tried to help their artist in the studio, but had seemingly endless patience with Keith's addictions. In 1984 and early '85, the label had released three Whitley singles, and none climbed any higher than number fifty-seven. Yet rather than drop him, RCA searched for new material and put Keith back in the studio. Soon after his wife walked out on him, Whitley scored with ''Miami, My Amy.'' In a very short time, it would become increasingly ironic that the song that had first been pitched by Dean Dillon to Lorrie Morgan, when they had both made their living in an Opryland bluegrass show, had put Keith Whitley on the map.

''Miami, My Amy'' would enter the playlists in November and remain on the charts for more than five months. It was a career-making record for Whitley. Suddenly the man who wondered if country radio would ever discover him was now all over the dial.

More than a decade after ''Miami, My Amy'' climbed the charts, Lorrie told *Country Weekly* about the first time she heard the recorded version of the song. She had been listening to the radio as she drove her car down a lightly travelled road when the song came on.

''I just pulled the car over and sat on the side of the

road," she recalled, "and said, 'Man, this is one of the best records I have ever heard.' "

That song, written by an old friend and coworker, would be her introduction to the man who would soon become the love of her life. To this day "Miami, My Amy" remains her favorite all-time country music single.

Within weeks of her first hearing the single on her car radio, she and Keith met backstage at the Opry, he had asked her for her phone number, and she had declined to give it to him. And the story could have ended right there, because at the time Lorrie was considering trying to get back together with her ex-husband in order to enhance her daughter's life.

Checking out of the Opry House and getting into her car, Morgan began to question why she was so scared of initiating a new relationship. If she had given Keith her number, then he might have called, and what was the harm in that? As she drove down the road, she began to wonder if it was too late to take advantage of this opportunity. Deciding that it wasn't, she turned around and headed back to the Opry.

When Lorrie returned to the Opry House, she gave a security guard her number and asked him to give that number to Whitley. Keith evidently got her note because he called the next morning. He missed Lorrie, she was at Mass, but he left a message. Lorrie got back to him when she returned home. After a few calls and some time together, the two became good friends. And when Whitley's divorce became final, they began dating. Their creative match seemed almost as perfect as their rapport in their private life. Many were figuring that even if the two singers' careers ended up going nowhere, their relationship would take them everywhere.

For Whitley, whose RCA products were now flying off the shelves, the road called often and so his days with the new love of his life were numbered. For Morgan, *Nashville Now*, the Opry, her daughter, and her bookings kept her on the move too.

A lot of the shows at which Lorrie was now working were benefits. These fund raisers were tying their sales directly to her exposure on *Nashville Now*. By and large ticket prices were cheap and the communities where Lorrie sang were small. But she still gave those fans everything she had. She did the Morgan name proud night after night.

While working in Nashville, she also performed at shows like the Music Valley Festival. Working at five in the afternoon during the last week in August, and then coming back for a second show at ten, was not easy. The heat and humidity were killers. Many wondered why she gave so much and worked so hard. After all, in reality, this was just a minor showcase. The festival wasn't even charging admission, so how important could it be? Yet George had taught Lorrie that every show, no matter how small, was the most important show she would ever do. So she treated even the tiniest venue and each seemingly insignificant fan as if they were special. Still, even for an entertainer's entertainer, it had to be hard to push on when the numbers were small. Some also felt that it must have been difficult to be falling in love with someone who was so hot when she was not.

While Keith was singing at some of the country's best venues, Lorrie was performing in places like Lebanon, Tennessee. While Whitley was wowing crowds who had gathered to party, Morgan was playing before groups who were raising money for organizations like the Sherriff's Youth Ranch. While Keith worked with some really big names, Lorrie often performed with a cast that included Mike Snider, Tom Grant, and Norm ''Killer'' Fraser, names not known very far outside of the influence of TNN. While Keith was creating his own excitement with his own music, Lorrie's shows were often an extension of *Nashville Now* taken on the road. And while Keith was the hottest new sound on the market and had the young country fans going wild, Lorrie was still viewed in large part as a cable television personality who mainly registered with the grandparents of the young country fans. They were a couple made up of two individuals headed in different directions.

Lorrie should have probably felt frustrated about this,

but she didn't seem to. She loved watching Keith's career blossom and she didn't have room in her life for jealousy. Besides, she had the security of having remained true to herself and her ideals. And the importance of this strength of character that she felt was such an important part of her life was reinforced every time she appeared at the Opry. Here her values were always appreciated and her talents were never taken for granted.

When Lorrie wasn't working onstage or being a devoted mother, she could now be found writing for Acuff-Rose. Even when MCA had given up on her as an artist, her first employer had decided that it was time to give Morgan a second look as a writer. In many ways, maybe due in part to the incredible talent she saw in Whitley, her writing was the one thing that she genuinely wanted to improve. Like her songwriting father, Lorrie wanted to be able to take her own thoughts, ideas, and experiences, and shape them into music and lyrics that would touch people's hearts. She worked long and hard at developing this skill. Someday, she must have vowed, she would write her own timeless classic.

Going inside herself to discover the essence of her own thoughts, beliefs, and ideas may have been one of the most important steps Morgan could make at this time. Even though she didn't know it, she was about to begin a wild and unpredictable journey that would have more ups and downs than an Opryland roller coaster. She was about to touch both heaven and hell at the same time. She was about to know great joy and sadness all at once. She was about to experience moments that few would ever want to experience and even fewer could survive. A mighty and tragic adventure was just ahead, and taking stock of herself, getting to know her strengths and placing her feet on solid ground, was probably the only thing that could have begun to prepare her for what was just around life's corner.

Chapter 7

It had now been over a decade since George Morgan had passed away, and to many it seemed as if his daughter was no closer to following in her father's footsteps as a successful recording artist than she was on the day the Opry giant died. Four chances had been given to Lorrie by three different labels, and none of them had panned out. Yet all was not bleak for the twenty-six-year-old Opry member. Even though her career might have been on a downward spiral, she was in love. And when a person is in love it seems that it doesn't take much to make that person happy.

By mid-summer Keith had recorded his first top-ten song, "Ten Feet Away." The song's title pretty much described how close a long line of prospective suitors could get to Lorrie Morgan. In Music City, it was an established fact that Lorrie was now dating Keith exclusive of everyone else. He was the only man in her life. And whenever they were seen together—be it at a concert date, a restaurant, or the Opry—they wore a look of a couple very much in love.

Lorrie told her friends and fans that she had never been happier. She thought that Keith was the best thing that had ever happened to her. And for the first time ever, she seemed to be putting her own career on the back burner for a man. Yet behind the façade of the Cinderella tale, there was a dark side. And though Lorrie didn't talk about it in public, even while she was falling head over heels in love with Whitley, she was also beginning to experience some of the hell that this young man lived with on a daily basis.

Morgan had heard about Whitley's problems with

booze even as she began to go out with him. She had been warned by people who cared about her that loving this man might bring pain. Yet Lorrie might have felt that her experiences with George Jones had prepared her for what she would come up against with Keith. And more importantly, at first, Lorrie just didn't see much that indicated that the new man in her life was dependent upon this liquid drug. He didn't drink at all when he was with her. She had never even seen him take a sip of alcohol. So she could naturally assume that there was not much about which to worry.

All that changed one night when she went to see him at his home. Upon arriving she didn't find the happy-go-lucky smiling singer who usually greeted her. Instead she found Keith drunk and unconscious. When she couldn't bring him to, she called in help. It was then determined that Whitley had consumed so much alcohol that it seemed best to get to a medical facility. Lorrie decided to rush him to the Vanderbilt Hospital Emergency room. Their personnel went to work not just sobering him up, but saving his life. A shocked Morgan discovered that the singer had very nearly drunk himself to death. He suffered severe alcohol poisoning. When the emergency staff finally were convinced that he was out of danger, the attending doctors told Morgan that Whitley shouldn't have lived through this binge. It seemed that Keith's blood/alcohol level was the highest that they had ever seen in the long history of Vanderbilt. Anyone else who had come in with this level of alcohol in his bloodstream had been dead on arrival. They warned Keith and Lorrie that Whitley was going to have to get things under control or die. Keith assured them that he understood and that he would be careful.

Over the course of the next few months, most days were good. Many days went by and Whitley wouldn't drink at all. As a matter of fact, Morgan informed friends that she never saw him take even a single drink. Yet even in the midst of all the good times, on several more occasions, Lorrie would run by to see Keith and find him passed out. Then they would repeat the trip to the emergency room. After he sobered up, Whitley would again be sorry and promise to get his act together.

A wise person would have probably written Whitley off as an exercise in futility. He had an obvious problem that Lorrie didn't seem to be able to help him to control. Still, even as she watched him waste his life time and time again, she was ever the more drawn to him, ever the more aware of how much he had to give. So, try as she could, she couldn't help falling in love with him.

As summer turned to fall and Lorrie and Keith spent more and more hours together, the woman felt that it was time to make the big step. Maybe if he was married to her, maybe if their lives were bonded together, then maybe she could offer him the strength he needed to stay away from alcohol. After all, couldn't real love cure anything?

RCA released Keith's "Homecoming '63" in early November. The video, which showed a high school twenty-year reunion, featured Lorrie as Keith's wife. On November 22, 1986, the two got married in real life. Though the song would stall at number nine, the marriage seemed headed for the top spot.

Few couples in Nashville seemed more in love than Lorrie and Keith. She was devoted to him, he was so good to her, and even Lorrie's daughter from her former marriage loved her new daddy. The public relations department at RCA cheered this good news. Just as Whitley was becoming one of the hottest properties in Music City, this highly publicized union between the artist and the second generation Opry member seemed to be this era's version of Johnny Cash and June Carter. It was great P.R. It was made to order for magazines and newspapers. And an up-and-coming artist couldn't receive too much good news. No career had ever suffered from too many features on happiness and love.

Many of those who knew of Keith's darker side were hoping that Johnny and June, a couple mentioned from time to time in stories on the Whitleys, would be the model for this union. Cash had come into his life with Carter carrying extreme addictions. He too had been a tortured genius. He too led a lifestyle that almost killed him. Yet his love of June and her devotion to him had helped him escape the deadly shackles of drug abuse. Maybe, many prayed, God had put Keith with Lorrie for the same purpose. They knew that he needed a miracle and they hoped that this miracle was the love of a woman.

In public it appeared that these two would bring out the best in each other. Keith loved Lorrie so much that he even went through the red tape to adopt her daughter from her first marriage. And just as he was preparing to become Morgan's father, Lorrie informed him that the two of them were going to have their own child too. As his seventh RCA single, "Hard Livin' " climbed the charts, it appeared that nothing could detour Whitley's trip to the top or the young family's shot at real happiness. And nothing the fans knew about could.

No one could say that Whitley wasn't trying hard to get his life together. For that effort, and a thousand other reasons, Lorrie loved Keith as she had no man. And he treated her right too. He would give her cards, flowers, and gifts and make her believe that she was a princess. She even related to several interviewers, "Keith treated me like a queen. In the three years we were married, he never said one ugly word to me, never raised his voice."

Lorrie also assured her friends that Whitley loved her more than anything else in his life. Yet even though she knew this was true, she also recognized that something he hated would sometimes pull him away from her. In order to make sure that it didn't take him away forever, Lorrie went through their home with a fine tooth comb and trashed all the booze. This seemingly simple act didn't begin and end with getting rid of the liquor cabinet, it just started there. As she searched their home, Lorrie found alcohol hidden under things, behind things and in things in almost every part of their home.

Through hard work and perseverance, the first six months of their union were almost perfect and Keith appeared to have things almost in control. It was the almost that was killing Lorrie. Though he never drank around

Morgan, he would still sometimes hit the bottle when he was away from home. Lorrie would get calls in the middle of the night from friends telling her that Keith was drunk and at a certain location. When she could, she would pick him up and bring him home. On nights he was gone and she didn't get any calls, Lorrie would pace the floor deeply concerned that her husband would kill himself or someone else in a car accident.

"I was always afraid of leaving him (to even go work a show)," she told *Country Music Magazine* after she had lost him. "I was afraid of what leaving would do to him. I knew that when I was there, I could take care of him." Yet when she was on the road or he was on the road, she worried constantly that he was losing control. Many days she would call him a half-dozen times just to make sure he was all right.

When they had the opportunity to work together, Lorrie watched fans try to get in good with Keith by handing him a drink or some drugs before or after the shows. When she was there, he tossed them away. Yet she told her friends that she wondered if he had the strength when she was away from him to get rid of them. It was the shows where she didn't work with him that kept Lorrie up late at night.

After a while, Lorrie came to realize that even her love couldn't help Keith conquer all of his inner demons. And as she learned more about his background, she must have begun to understand just how helpless she was.

Whitley was no newcomer to drinking. He had a long history of alcohol abuse, one that had almost cost him his life in automobile accidents on several occasions. At age seventeen, he and a friend had gotten drunk and decided to see how fast their car could go. Soon after they hit 120 miles per hour, they lost control. Keith's friend died.

This brush with death should have opened his eyes to his problem, but it didn't. Even though he had learned firsthand the dangers of alcohol, he kept drinking more and more. Two years after that first accident, Whitley was drinking and driving and again lost control of the car while going at a high speed. This time he ended up flying off a cliff and into a stream. How he lived through the crash no one knew, why he hadn't drowned was anyone's guess. And he didn't stop.

Though incredibly talented, his drinking had long hindered his career. When he first recorded in Nashville as a solo artist, he was often so drunk he couldn't even slur the words together, remember the lyrics to songs he had written, or stay awake for any more than a few takes at a time. RCA, which had stuck with him through some very bleak times, was ready to cut him loose altogether if he hadn't gotten his act together on his third album. And for a while, it appeared as though he had buried the demons. Finally a sober Whitley produced work that began to really reflect his tremendous potential.

Yet even when he was at his best, things often didn't seem right in Keith's world. As talented as he was, as loving as he was, he was also sometimes uncomfortable with himself. Many times he would drink to fight off the loneliness and doubts, even though it seemed that his world was filled with people who loved him. Why should he be so depressed? people asked. To them, it seemed as if he had everything

Yet what most didn't seem to realize was that Whitley was a true alcoholic. He simply couldn't drink a single drink without needing more and more. Once he started, he couldn't stop. He craved booze and craved it in large amounts.

It didn't take long for Lorrie to realize that any form of alcohol was a poison for her husband. She was also concerned that the very men who her husband seemed to admire the most had experienced the same problem. The critics could look at Keith's idols and see their influence on his music. Lorrie could look at them and see their influence on Keith's life.

Whitley revered Lefty Frizzell, George Jones, and Hank Williams more than he did anyone else. Two of those three greats, Lefty and Hank, had died early due in some or large part to their well-publicized thirst for booze. This liquid had robbed them of everything from self-respect to old age. It had cost them almost everyone who was dear to them. It had seen them drummed out of the Nashville establishment. Time and time again, both of the country music stars had admitted that they hated what it was doing to them, but their bodies' needs always overruled their judgment. They drank until they died.

Meanwhile, George Jones, the only living member of Whitley's trio of heroes, had almost allowed alcohol to not only steal his career, but almost everything else he had too.

Lorrie had seen the results of Jones's addictions up close. She just couldn't allow the love of her life to end up like Frizzell, Williams, and Jones. She was not going to let Keith give up his life and career without a fight. With that in mind, was it any wonder that in a very real sense, her family was now her entire focus?

In June 1987, the annual Lorrie Morgan fan club breakfast at Fan Fair turned into a baby shower. Lorrie and Keith were expecting their child within the week. A very ripe Lorrie was glowing as fans brought her gifts and wished her well. Yet even as the group of more than 150 gathered at the Sheraton Hotel South laughed, shared stories, and prepared for the new birth, Lorrie and her fan club president Wanda Anderson announced that they wanted to see something else special happen very soon. They wanted Lorrie's fans to help raise the money to have a star installed in honor of George Morgan at the Country Music Hall of Fame. Yet even as she publicly cried out for country music to recognize her father's immense contributions, she privately cried out for her husband to beat his demons and recognize just how much she needed him sober and happy.

Outwardly Keith appeared wonderful. His work in the studio was the best he had ever done. RCA was confident that he would soon replace Randy Travis as the next huge country star. About the only thing the singer seemed concerned about was being a new father. Whitley who hardly ever seemed nervous on stage, admitted to almost everyone that he was nervous about this baby. Yet as he and Lorrie dueted for a Fan Fair crowd on "I Just Want

You'' and "That's the Way Love Goes," the fans couldn't help but believe that Whitley's life and this union seemed to be on solid ground.

At the close of the festivities, a genuinely touched Lorrie thanked her most loyal fans for their support. "I haven't been on TV that much the past seven or eight months," she had explained. "I've been taking time off until the baby comes. But I did just finish some vocals yesterday on a new recording session." In other words, she was asking those who loved her not to give up on her. And she had promised that when they got together at her fan club breakfast the following year, she would have more to show than just a one-year-old child. Something would be going on with her career too, she assured them.

Her manager, Jack McFadden, seemed to agree that the best was just arriving. Yet for now, things were much more focused on a baby than they were a career. And it was WSM DJ Keith Bilbrey who upon examining the various baby gifts the couple had received told writer Robert K. Oermann, "I'd give anything to have Lorrie Morgan rock and sing me to sleep." Bilbrey may have meant the comment as a joke, but Morgan was hoping that her husband could give up alcohol so that he could help her rock their child too.

On June 15, the Whitleys welcomed Jesse, a son. The birth made news around the country, but nowhere was it more celebrated that at the Opry. The Opry's special child had produced another little one for them to spoil backstage. In the Morgan family, this was becoming a tradition.

Lorrie was drawn to motherhood, and even though she had promised her manager and fans that she was going to get busy soon, she actually tried to slow down even more. She wanted to stay home, not just to take care of the baby and Morgan, but to be with Keith. Yet even as she wasn't really pushing it, her career was now beginning to make some waves.

Many were shocked when they discovered that for the first time since she was a child, performing was not the end all for Lorrie. It almost didn't seem to matter. She was getting used to staying home and just being a wife and mother. Yet even as these roles had come to mean so much to her, Keith urged her back to performing. He didn't want her to lose her edge. He wanted her to get back on the road and out with the fans. He wanted her to live up to her potential just like she wanted him to reach his.

When she finally did hit the road after having the child, Whitley would call after each show and asked Lorrie how she did. He wanted to know the songs that she had used, how the audience responded to each of them, and what she had done differently from the last show. He pushed her to put more emotion into each set. Through encouragement, he made her better. He forced her to think of every song as an audition for a record contract. And this coaching was paying off too. As she would say, "He gave me reason to sing again." Suddenly her fire to be a star had come back, and she credited her husband with fueling this desire.

During a typical concert set at the time, Ms. Morgan and her band Something Special would churn out classics such as "Stand by Your Man," "Crazy," "C.C. Ryder," and harkening back to the days of her early youth, the Beatles's "Eight Days a Week." Completely at ease with her crowds, she joked, laughed, and allowed them to mix in questions and comments. It seemed that her love for Keith and his pride in her stage work had even taken away a bit of her shyness.

From time to time, if he could work it out, Keith would join her onstage for a number like "That's the Way Love Goes." In the spotlight, the two seemed to not only perform as one, but enjoy the fact that they were a couple sharing in something they both loved. To many it seemed that Lorrie had never enjoyed what she was doing as much as now. The fans just knew that she had found the one love of her life. Yet even in the midst of the informal love fest that these small concert gatherings usually became, Lorrie always remembered to mention another man besides her husband. Each night she would break with everything else at least once and tell a host of fans who were too young to know or too young to remember George Morgan, the story of the greatest man she knew. And near the end of each show, she would always do her version of her dad's biggest and most beloved hit, "Candy Kisses."

MCA may have preferred that fans know the singer as *Nashville Now*'s Lorrie Morgan when Lorrie had recorded for the label. But now that she was on her own, she was heralded as the *Grand Ole Opry Star* Lorrie Morgan. To be as young as she was and have this time-honored label attached to her name gave her a sense of importance and status that no other up-and-coming young female act could claim. And she sensed that even younger fans were beginning to attach a degree of significance to the Opry membership and what it stood for.

Yet even though she embraced being an Opry star, Lorrie still didn't have a strong musical identity. With no hits of her own, she was forced into doing other people's classics. Yet even though she could sing them well, sometimes even better than those who had taken them up the charts, she needed more than just other people's classics to move from the small-time to the mainstream.

So even as Lorrie was involving herself in "Dreammakers," a group that helped fulfill the wishes of very sick or dying children, and even as Keith hit number one with "Don't Close Your Eyes," Lorrie was closing her eyes and making a wish. A few months before she had just wanted to be a mother and wife. Now with Keith's urging, she wished that she could get into the studio another time. She wanted another crack at getting radio interested in her product.

As Lorrie continued to improve her live act, many long-time country music writers and performers noted that she was now following in her father's footsteps in more ways that just music. George Morgan had earned the reputation as one of the nicest stars in the business. He always went the extra mile for his fans. He would stay after shows and talk and sign autographs for hours. Now, when few artists did any more than run out and sing then run back to the bus, Lorrie was pressing flesh with the patrons. And her fans loved her for it. And this base, which had once been so small, was now growing and beginning to shake up radio stations with requests for her music. The stations couldn't give the fans's requests any air time because they had no Morgan singles. When the outcry grew loud enough, some of the jocks began asking the label representatives why Lorrie Morgan wasn't under contract.

Feeling ready to try it against Reba and a new crop of female singers, Lorrie was growing more frustrated than even her fans with her inability to land a record deal. Her manager, Jack McFadden, was going door to door calling Lorrie the ''best-kept secret in Nashville.'' Yet Jack, her fans, and the interested disc jockeys couldn't seem to drum up enough interest to make a record company jump. Everyone knew Lorrie, everyone liked Lorrie, but no one seemed too excited by Lorrie.

''It was hard to get taken seriously because I was around so much,'' Lorrie later recalled. ''I was always George's little girl. I guess that's what happens when everybody knows you while you're growing up.'' At that time being George's little girl didn't mean much except to country music's older generation of fans, but being Keith Whitley's wife just might be something worth noting. At least Keith thought so.

When he wasn't on the road or in the studio, Keith was pushing his wife to the various labels. Time and time again, he beat his head against the wall trying to convince someone that Lorrie could really sing. Finally as he grew into one of RCA's most important acts, he got the company to give his wife another chance. They may have acted first as a favor to Whitley, but ultimately RCA would discover that they were doing themselves a huge favor.

''I thought to myself,'' Lorrie explained about getting the deal, '' 'This is the last time I'm going to try this.' I was working the road, doing the Nashville Network, playing the Grand Ole Opry, and still doing some demo sessions and writing, and I knew there would be one more opportunity for a record label to come my way. Had RCA not accepted that session, I wasn't sure what I was going to do, but I wasn't going to get turned down anymore.''

Just before RCA had called, Lorrie had really been ready to quit. She told Keith that she just wanted to give up and be a writer, wife, and mother. Yet McFadden and Whitley wouldn't let her. Keith even told her that she would hate herself if she didn't continue to plug away. He was right too. Ever since that first night on the Opry, Lorrie had known that performing was what she wanted to do with her life. So if she had been honest with herself, she would have realized that she couldn't quit. By the same token, she didn't know if she could face failure again either.

With his full support, Morgan followed in the footsteps of her hot husband and joined the stable of Nashville's most important label. From the first day at RCA, she noticed a big difference in this company and all the others who had produced her in the past. The first and most important thing she encountered was honesty.

At RCA she would begin her relationship by being introduced to producer Barry Beckett. Beckett, who had worked with the likes of Hank Williams, Jr. and Alabama, hadn't liked Morgan's earlier stuff and he told her so. He said that he hadn't liked her recordings because he believed that she hadn't really sold herself in the studio. He didn't think there was any heart in her music simply because she hadn't been a big enough part of picking it out.

Lorrie didn't respond well to Barry's critique. She admitted later that she wanted to either get up and walk out or hit him. Instead she bit her lip and stayed to listen to what he had to say.

The next time Beckett and Morgan met, he played a video of some of Lorrie's past performances of her live appearances on *Nashville Now*. He showed her how good she sounded when she was selling her material to a live audience. Then he pointed out that in the past, on her recordings, she simply hadn't projected that kind of raw emotion. Now Morgan was beginning to understand what Beckett was trying to get her to understand. He loved her voice, he thought she had tremendous potential, he liked her live work, he just thought the past efforts that record producers had made hadn't captured that. He wanted to.

With that in mind, Beckett brought the singer in to his office, let her listen to the demos, and together they picked out what sounded good—the kind of stuff that she could sing with fever and emotion. Suddenly, as the studio work began, as if by magic, Lorrie came alive. Even in the studio with no audience in sight, it now sounded as if Morgan was singing for her fans. Now that was the way George would have done it!

MCA and Hickory hadn't given Lorrie this kind of tough love, nor had they allowed her any room to pick her own material or get emotionally involved in what she was recording. Lorrie now realized she simply hadn't cared much for what her other labels had chosen for her to record. This had been reflected in the final product. Barry had given her a voice in every element of the production so that she could find vehicles for that voice. It was a fifty-fifty deal in finding songs and selecting arrangements. Barry got the chance to see how she responded to every facet of the process. And now the producer could see that Lorrie was excited about being a recording artist!

Lorrie had long said that she couldn't sing things she hadn't experienced. Her music was from the heart, not from the imagination, she had explained. Barry allowed her to see with her heart, and with that in mind she began to understand what it took to really deliver a song with hit potential.

One of the songs the team picked out had been a previous cut by Pam Tillis. "Five Minutes" offered Lorrie a chance to take a sure hit that had been missed by Tillis's label and put her own spin on it. What Pam's company hadn't heard, Lorrie did. She knew with "Five Minutes" she'd make some magic on her own. Barry and Lorrie weren't going to miss with this overlooked hit,

and neither was RCA. Nor was the label going to over-
look their newest artist.

"I felt like a veteran as far as being in the studio,"
Lorrie remembered as they wrapped that first effort, "but
I was really nervous about being a new artist of RCA.
There was a lot of pressure because it was my first album,
and I knew Nashville and the people in the business were
going to be very eager to critique it." She could have
also been nervous because she realized that these people
really cared about her and she didn't want to let them
down.

Barry decided to use Lorrie's emotions and strong vocal talents as the vehicle to carry this effort. So by and
large, the album was made up of very strong ballads. Yet
when it came time to showcase Morgan for the very first
time on a single, the label decided to do it with an up-
tempo sound.

As the year wound down, RCA released what would
be her most important single to date, "Trainwreck of
Emotion," and for the first time in four years Lorrie was
on the charts. Helped in part by a strong video, Morgan
lasted almost five months on the playlists, finally peaking
at number twenty. It was ironic that this song and the
video that went with it, had established her as a star,
because Lorrie had really wanted to pass on "Trainwreck" the first time she heard it.

Lorrie felt that train songs were a man's domain. Besides, she reasoned, train songs had been out of style on
the hit parade since the time when the list was actually
referred to as the hit parade. No one did them anymore.
Most of the fans who were buying country music now
had never even ridden a train. Who would identify with
it? Her producer and label believed that millions would.
And besides, wasn't a second-generation country music
performer the perfect person to put train songs back in
style? And if RCA's promise to Lorrie to allow her to
come alive with emotion in the studio was to make good,
then why not spell that out in the title on their initial
release!

As Lorrie rode a trainwreck that as soon it had left the

station seemed headed for fame, Keith's career surged too. His "Don't Close Your Eyes" album produced a number of major hits, including 1988's biggest smash, "When You Say Nothing at All." Yet as it turned out, as Whitley surged into the forefront of country music, as all of his dreams appeared within easy reach, as the love of his life gave him a son that he spoiled every chance he got, he continued to wrestle with the invisible demons that had plagued him for so long. Even though few around him knew just how bad things had gotten, a lot of his friends seemed to sense that there was a sad urgency in his eyes. They wondered why—why would a man so close to having everything be running from the devil?

Even in the midst of a career that was taking more and more of his time, Keith spent hours with his new son. They rode on his motorcycle, shared breakfast, and sang little songs. Some of his friends felt that through Jesse, Lorrie, and Morgan, the singer would find something stronger to hold onto than a bottle. And so much of the time he did.

Yet even though much of his life was on the upswing, Keith couldn't seem to lose his need for booze. He was now back to trying to hide bottles around the house. At times, Lorrie became so desperate that she would literally tie the two of them together as they slept in an attempt to keep him from sneaking away in the middle of the night to drink. Yet she couldn't be there all the time. Now she had a career to push too.

In 1995, Lorrie told Dick Zimmerman, the esteemed entertainment writer of *USA Today*, "There's a time when it's harder on the person who isn't the alcoholic, when you have to sit up and you've got kids to take care of and they've got school. Sometimes, you've just got to get some rest, and that was the only way I could find to get any rest (tying the two of them together)."

When Whitley could slip away and drink, he would do so with a vengeance. He could go from cold sober to completely wasted in half an hour. He had come back from very short breaks at recording sessions drunk, when just a few minutes before he had been completely lucid. Yet by and large, he hid his drinking from everyone, even Lorrie when he could. He usually drank alone. And he lied to himself about his problem. He kept telling himself and those around him that he was about to get things under control. And he would then say that his wife was the reason he had to clean up his life. Yet he must have known that he was walking on dangerous ground by the mere fact that he was in such a state of denial. In Lorrie's own words, he was a "ticking time bomb."

Lorrie and Keith had bought a home together. She had hoped that this new setting would give her husband a new lease on life. As always, for a while it did. Then Lorrie would find him going through the medicine cabinet reading labels and looking for anything that had alcohol in it. Lectures, prayers, tough love, unconditional love, and a thousand other ways of getting through to Keith were tried again and again. Yet none of these seemed to get to the heart of the problem. He had a disease and when he should have been on top of the world, Keith was drowning in a sea of need for poison.

Not long after they had settled into their new home, Keith had discovered that Lefty Frizzell's grave was just a few minutes away. Lefty had abused alcohol for almost all of his life, but, just like in Keith's case, that abuse hadn't been able to totally hide his brilliant musical gifts. His biggest hit, "If You've Got the Money, I've Got the Time," was still a country music anthem. Yet the talented honky-tonk artist had died at the early age of forty-seven due in large part to his affair with the bottle.

From the first time he visited the scene, Keith felt drawn to Lefty's grave. Whitley spent so much time there that some of his friends felt the singer had made it into a shrine. Yet in spite of this quirky action, and in spite of his occasional drinking binges, on the surface most things appeared to be better than they ever had been before. Keith seemed to want to be happy a lot worse than he wanted to bury his pain.

Lorrie would remember these days almost a year later while visiting her father's hometown of Barberton, Ohio.

She would tell writer Lori Noernberg, "His disease was uncontrollable, but you couldn't have asked for a better man, father, and husband than Keith Whitley."

She added, "It's a sad thing, Keith didn't want to drink. He liked being sober, he loved his family, his wife, and kids."

Country music is filled with songs about relationships where love just didn't seem to be enough to make happy endings. Sadly, country music was about to discover that from time to time, the lyrics of those songs were true.

Chapter 8

By the beginning of 1989, Keith had decided to talk with the public and the press about his problems with alcohol. He seemed to want to admit that he knew that he was an alcoholic. He also seemed to want to apologize for anyone who had been hurt or let down by his bouts with booze. He also let on that he was getting things under control and that Lorrie was the main reason he was gaining that control. In a sense, now that the rumors were out, he didn't want to look like another George Jones. He also wanted to reassure his fans and his label that he was going to put his problems behind him.

Whitley probably really believed that he was in the midst of controling the substance abuse that had controlled his life for so long. Yet in reality he was just lying to himself. He simply couldn't do it without professional help, and he didn't have time to take off from a career that was as hot as his was. So, as much as he wanted to quit, it seemed that the beckoning calls of the alcohol were even stronger. So while those around him began to relax a bit and think that maybe he was going to be able to handle things, he still was a lot shakier than anyone knew. Though he appeared healthy, and this in spite of the fact that he was smoking at least three packs of cigarettes a day, he was still on the edge between walking away from his problems and drowning in them.

Musically, Keith's latest release, ''I'm No Stranger to the Rain,'' was on its way to becoming one of the most sensational singles in Nashville. Critics loved it, fans couldn't get enough of it, and it would be the perfect follow-up record to ''Don't Close Your Eyes.'' This single would finally and solidly establish Whitley as one of

Nashville's most important acts. No longer was Keith a star in the making, he was a powerhouse. RCA was assured that this man would be spinning hits for a long time to come.

Yet the dark shadows in his life were still there. For some reason, his self-confidence still suffered. Even as he talked about living in the light, he seemed drawn to the night. It was almost as if he had a horrible appointment looming ahead that he had to keep no matter what the cost.

While in retrospect it is easy to see just how hard Lorrie had worked to get Keith's life in order, what few realized at this time was that he also helped her put life into perspective. Lorrie had long stressed on small things, and her husband helped her see the big picture. He showed her that every headache was not a brain tumor and every stomachache was not cancer. He got her to see that every little thing that got in the way of making an appointment or getting her hair fixed was easy to deal with and even easier to laugh off. Keith taught Lorrie that she could handle anything with grace and style and nothing could or should ruffle her feathers. This had been a big reason that Lorrie had been able to let go and finally enjoy what was happening in her own professional life.

Yet as much promise as she felt she had at this moment, even with "Trainwreck of Emotion" climbing the charts and becoming one of CMT's most requested videos, even with RCA behind her 100 percent, even with as many great stories that were being written in the press about her, Lorrie still questioned if her career was really going to explode like the writers promised. The fact was that the road still didn't always offer her the ray of sunshine she needed on the gloomy days before she finally hit her stride. And this lack of success was not something she could blow off. She had to worry about it no matter how much Keith told her not to.

In Paducah, Kentucky she played a show to just over 100 people. Lorrie worked that crowd hard and they loved her, but was a handful of fans worth giving up precious time with her children and her husband? Maybe, she thought, when people heard her first album, things will be different. Maybe then she will be appreciated by a whole new group of fans. Still, she wondered and fretted.

The project to which RCA and Lorrie had dedicated so much of the last half of 1988 had a great deal of promise. Yet a lot of Music City projects that had shown great promise had never become successful. Until *Leave Your Light On* hit the streets and fans began to believe in it the way that Lorrie did, it was just so much hot air. Yet the initial word back from the press indicated that playing before small crowds was about to become a thing of the past for Lorrie Morgan.

The New York *Daily News* said that *Leave Your Light On* would "catapult" the singer to stardom. If it did, then maybe a host of folks would note whom Lorrie had thanked for this project on the liner notes. Lorrie wanted the world to know just how much she appreciated the contributions her husband had made in helping her to grow to meet this opportunity. In those liner notes, she foremost thanked Keith for "teaching me how to sing with heart and giving me reason to (sing)."

The Nashville *Tennessean* also chimed in with strong support after they heard an advance copy of the product. The local Music City voice wrote, "She (Lorrie) has a smoky, torrid vocal quality that seems to work equally well on pop-tinged ballads and gut-bucket honky-tonk blues." Other great reviews followed. The usually critical press seemed to think that even with her first album that this singer had already hit full stride. She wasn't just learning how to walk, they indicated through their praise, she was already running. As it turned out, soon her record would be joining her in full race form.

In this case, the press had been right. *Leave the Light On* left the record vendors in record numbers. Within a year, the album had racked up more than 750,000 in sales (it would stay on the charts for eighty-four weeks). This would become the mother of Morgan's recording career as five singles would jump into the top ten from this one product. What a way to begin with a major label! Of course, this overnight success had really begun more than two decades before, this in spite of the fact that Lorrie wasn't even thirty years old.

As Lorrie began to work to larger and larger crowds, she began to really play up her next single. She wanted the next release to make it into the top ten, something that "Trainwreck of Emotion" had missed by ten spots. Morgan figured that to really be taken seriously "Dear Me" was going to have to be a major hit.

Lorrie had discovered "Dear Me" a decade before, but no one at her other labels would take seriously the chances of her making the song a hit. Still, she hadn't forgotten what she thought was one of the most beautiful compositions she had ever heard. When she was assisting in picking out material for her first RCA album, she played it for Barry Beckett. The producer not only loved it, but believed that this was a song that Lorrie's torchy vocal style could sell better than anyone in town. He not only gave her the thumbs up to use it on the album, but he recognized that this number was going to make an outstanding single.

Beginning from the day of its release in April, "Dear Me" would become Lorrie's most requested number to date. Fans who caught in on the radio loved it. Folks who saw the hauntingly beautiful black-and-white video couldn't get enough of it. And those fans who bought tickets to hear Lorrie sing it live were enraptured.

Vince Hoffard of the Carbondale-Herrin, Illinois, *Southern Illinoisan* may have picked up on just how good Lorrie was about to become even before most of the national media and the Music City establishment took note. After hearing her efforts on "Dear Me" and the rest of the cuts from *Leave the Light On* and catching her in concert, Hoffard wrote, "As a vocalist Morgan is pure power. She belts out a vast range of vibrant lyrics, from slow ballads to rambunctious up-tempo verses. She is a worthy replacement for Brenda Lee as the new *Little Miss Dynamite.*"

Lorrie and Hoffard had talked between one of her two southern Illinois shows, and the writer was quite taken

One of country music's sexiest women.
(*Photo © by Vicki Houston*)

Ducking out of the Opryland Hotel after a 1995 performance for the Country Radio Seminar.
(Photo © Vicki Houston)

In the tradition of her great father, George, night after night Lorrie gives the fans everything she has.
(Photo © Vicki Houston)

Lorrie with John Randall, then boyfriend and now husband, at the TNN Music City New Awards in 1997.
(Photo © Vicki Houston)

A solid athlete, Lorrie looks great after finishing a charity softball game.
(Photo © Vicki Houston)

An entertainer who does it all performing at the RCA show at Fan Fair. *(Photo © Vicki Houston)*

Lorrie onstage with Mike Love, Brian Wilson and the Beach Boys. *(Photo © Vicki Houston)*

The late Keith Whitley: incredible talent, tragic life.
(Photo © Vicki Houston)

A fan favorite since her teens, Lorrie has pulled down top
honors at the TNN Music City Awards many times including 1994 when she posed for this picture.
(Photo © Vicki Houston)

A third generation of Morgans and second generation of Whitleys joins his mother onstage at the Opry House.
(Photo © Vicki Houston)

by the singer. Yet as they visited, he couldn't help but note a couple of things that didn't seem to go with a performer who glowed with so much confidence on stage. One was the way that Lorrie nervously puffed on cigarette after cigarette as if something was bothering her deeply. Yet in retrospect, it was the other interruption in their visit that seemed to present a strange bit of fore-shadowing.

Hoffard wrote in his article that every few minutes Lorrie would stop their interview and make futile at-tempts to get a hold of her husband via the phone. To the writer, it seemed strange that the singer/wife would go to such great lengths to track down a husband who was performing a few hundred miles away in Joplin, Mis-souri. Yet Lorrie continued to call and call. Little could Hoffard have realized that Morgan probably was doing more than just checking in for an "I love you."

Lorrie would later admit that she felt that something was eating at Keith and she didn't know what it was. Their life together was good, his career had never been better, but there was something deep down that was caus-ing him to worry and she couldn't get at it. She would later tell a host of friends and reporters, "The last few months he seemed to be looking for ways to get in trou-ble."

As Lorrie was interviewed in Illinois, doing a show in Alabama, or even as she cleaned the house in Tennessee, she had reason to worry. Keith was becoming increas-ingly more erratic in his behavior. While he was telling members of the press he was cleaning up his act, he was falling off the wagon in a big way.

One day he left and no one knew where he was. Lorrie called everywhere. Finally she was notified by the police that he had gotten drunk, wrecked his Jeep, and was in a local hospital. She went immediately to be by his side, and when she could, she brought him home again. He promised to straighten up and fly right, and for a while it seemed like he did. But with Keith it seemed the stop-watch was always ticking.

In April, Keith and Lorrie were booked together for a

date in Knoxville. Lorrie got to open for her husband and then watch him. It was like a family reunion and second honeymoon all rolled into one. Everything seemed so right, yet for some reason there was always a cloud that was hanging just over the horizon. There was always a chance that Keith would trip and fall. And Lorrie was so worried that when he fell the next time that there would be no one there to pick him up. In Knoxville, as the two growing stars wowed the fans, things seemed so good. Lorrie wished that she and Keith could always tour together. It would make matters so much easier on both of them. As it turned out, that would be one of the couple's many unrealized dreams. This would be the last time the two would appear on the same bill.

RCA and Barry Beckett had chosen a wonderful single, "Out of Your Shoes," as the release that would follow "Dear Me." The latter was looking very strong even during its first few weeks of release. So there was every reason to believe that "Out of Your Shoes" was destined to be a major hit. Yet in many ways, Lorrie would have liked to have been in someone else's shoes as she approached what should have been the best spring of her life.

In the first week of May, Lorrie was scheduled to leave for a short tour to promote her album. She had misgivings that she couldn't explain about going on the very necessary press junket and concert tour. These feelings grew worse as she got on the plane and opened an envelope that Keith had given her. The card inside the envelope wished her well in a very sober and serious way. This was a radical departure from the messages Keith usually gave her. Normally his notes were romantic or funny. This card's words were so haunting that Lorrie considered coming home, but she didn't. In truth why should she have? What justification could there be? Keith had sounded great on the phone and seemed to have things well in hand at home. He had assured her that everything was all right and that she had a very important job to do for both of them. And he was right. Still, his words didn't help her keep from worrying about him.

Keith Whitley visited early the morning of May 9 with Lorrie's brother-in-law about motorcycles and fishing at his and Lorrie's home. The two men drank coffee, laughed, and made some plans. As the visit broke up, Keith was stone-cold sober and appeared extremely happy. It was as if he was in love with life and had everything to live for. Yet over the next few minutes, while he was alone with his thoughts, the old haunting shadows must have come creeping back into his life.

A time line from the day indicated that Keith called his mother a short time after Lorrie's sister's husband had left him. Rather than upbeat and glowing, Whitley was now suddenly despondent, worn out, and overwhelmed by the demands that had been thrust upon him. He talked about how his drinking was hurting so many people and ruining his life. It was just nine in the morning.

Sometime in the few minutes between the time that he had had coffee with the brother-in-law and the time he had called his mother, Keith had begun to drink. It must have seemed bizarre and ironic, even to Whitley, that as he explained to his mother what was causing all of his problems, he was doing the very thing that was ruining his life. Yet Keith didn't sound so strange that it caused a great deal of worry for his mother. She had heard him this way before, and he had always worked his way out of it one way or another. Who would have thought this time would have been any different?

Keith continued to drink after hanging up the phone. He also must have mixed the booze with cocaine and prescription painkillers, though no one knew where he got the drugs. Concerned, though he really had no reason to be, Lorrie's brother-in-law decided to check in on Whitley when he couldn't reach him by phone. Around noon he entered Lorrie and Keith's home and found the singer fully clothed in his bed. The visitor quickly discovered that Whitley wasn't just taking a midday nap. And this time there would be no chance to make an emergency trip to the hospital. It was too late. Keith had no pulse.

It had not taken Keith Whitley three hours to go from

being happy and exuberant about life to embracing a cold and unforgiving death. Medical examiners estimated that he had died alone at home maybe less than an hour after his last phone call to his mother. While it was amazing that he could consume enough during that time to kill himself, it was no wonder that he died. His blood alcohol count was almost five times over the legal limit, .477. Half of his blood was booze. Ironically Whitley's *I Wonder Do You Think of Me* album was just beginning a long ride up the charts. Sadly, millions thought of him over the next few days and weeks, but most were as lost as Lorrie would soon be to explain why he had drunk himself to death.

Lorrie had been on the way to Alaska when she got the news of her husband's death. Lorrie told Janet Varnum of the Stillwater *News-Press* a few months later, "I knew there was somewhat of a problem before I left. I didn't know it was as severe as it was. He was not depressed or suicidal. And I don't think he intended to die. I think he was trying to drink away some of the stress."

Stress, the very thing that Keith had tried to teach Lorrie how to handle, had somehow pushed him overboard. There was something in his life he simply couldn't handle and wouldn't share with his wife. And if he shared it with anyone else, no one had said anything to Lorrie or the family. Whatever the problems were, Keith evidently couldn't deal with it on his own.

Lorrie immediately came home to make the funeral arrangements. It was a very sad occasion, and mixed with the sadness was anger. A lot of fans, as well as some in the Music City establishment, were mad at Keith for doing this to Lorrie. They were also upset that he had wasted so much of his potential, cheated them out of so much of his greatness. It was sad enough when something like a plane crash had stilled Jim Reeves or Patsy Cline, but to have a bottle of booze take another country star was a crime. When they first heard the news over the radio and on the news, thousands of fans called stations saying that it had to be a mistake, a rumor, a made-up bit of gossip by a rag sheet. But it wasn't.

There was a song that Keith had written in the days before his death that many felt was one of his autobiographical best. Yet he never got the chance to record it. In a sense this song would signal once again not just Whitley's ability to wrap his pain in his music, but to also forecast his own demise. The song's title was "I've Done Everything Hank Did But Die." In the end, Keith could sadly even claim that. Just like Hank, he had abused his body and robbed the world of a life that was filled with so much talent and so many wonderful bits of joy.

The very nature of the death, the haunting aspect of it, the fact that Keith had a song, "I'm No Stranger to the Rain," that was about to go number one, probably caused even more people than usual to take an interest in the funeral. There was something morbid and fascinating about a talented young man who had such a promising career and such a beautiful and famous wife dying so tragically and so young. Though it might have surprised the press, as thousands of fans crowded the service and the grave side, many staying there all night long just to get a look at the casket and the singer's family, it shouldn't have. Whitley was on a roll. Or at least he had been. And this outpouring of mass grief clearly showed the success he had been promised in the near future. In one sense, this huge throng of fans was a great tribute, in another way it was almost a sick expression of people's dark and often psychotic fascination with death. Many left the funeral only to go by bars and toast their hero with the same substance that had killed him.

On Friday, when Lorrie wanted to go back to the grave, she couldn't because of the crush of people. It was no different on Saturday. She couldn't even visit her husband's final resting place to attempt to come to grips with her situation. Morgan's rising fame, as well as Whitley's now superstar status, had robbed her of the closing she needed in order to get on with her life. And soon a lot of people didn't want her to get on with her life either.

Once he had been placed in the ground, there were a host of folks who seemed ready to immediately blame Lorrie for Keith's death. They wanted to know why she had put her career ahead of him. Why did she leave a man like this with his problems? They didn't care that Keith had urged her on. That he had demanded that she mine her own talent. Those who pointed the fingers didn't recognize that for most of their three years together, Lorrie had cheated her own career because she was watching him, living for him, taking care of him and loving him. Those who were now blaming her also didn't know and didn't care about the guilt that Lorrie carried. It was very hard for her to come to grips with that fact that no one could be there for Keith all the time. Yet deep down, she had to know, and those who pointed fingers had to know, that if he had been scared into death, so scared that he had had to drown himself in alcohol so early in the morning, then what happened could have happened at any moment. Even when Lorrie was nearby in town.

In a very real sense those who were blaming Morgan didn't know much about Whitley's background. If they had, they might have realized that Lorrie coming into Keith's life may have actually given him three years that he otherwise wouldn't have had. Without her watching over him and loving him, the pressures might have even killed him sooner. Those who were pointing fingers and blaming Morgan should have been thanking her. Whitley's genius, which was stilled so soon, might never have surfaced at all without Lorrie standing by him through all those moments when anyone else would have walked away. Yet few seemed ready to see that, and the tabloids weren't going to write the story that way either. They preferred the tales that portrayed her as cold and heartless.

Deep inside Lorrie would later admit that she was very bitter because at least part of the blame for Keith's death had been placed on her when it should have been placed on some of the people within the industry. And those who were responsible would not only not fess up to it, they wouldn't even recognize it. Most of them were too busy blaming her.

Lorrie told *Country Music Magazine*, "There are people in this business who will push you until you drop dead, and then wonder what the hell happened to you. That's exactly what happened to Keith.''

For the widow with two children the questions that haunted her the most after ''Why did he do it?'' was if she had the strength to make it on her own. Could she pay the bills and raise the kids? Could she face the pressures of a growing career? Could she find the strength to go on? Even she didn't know, and she really wouldn't have the chance to find it out for a couple of years. Right now all she could do was struggle to pick up the pieces and tell her friends, ''Damn, I miss him.''

Lorrie had been scheduled to work the Grand Ole Opry the day after Keith had been buried. Many just assumed that she would cancel. Yet in Lorrie's mind, there was no question if she should go on. Most people who suffered great losses needed to feel the love and support of family. The Opry was where her family was. The performers, the stagehands, the musicians, and the fans, these people were the support group she needed. This was the church where she could once again find a bit of her faith. It was also a place where she could answer the most important questions about herself and her own life, ''Could she continue in the business that had contributed to the death of her father and her husband?''

The Opry show the day after the funeral answered the question of ''Could she go on?'' She had been nervous before her song, but the crowd had wrapped her in their arms and assured her that they loved her the moment she had been introduced. Even though it was extremely difficult and took every bit of strength she could muster, Lorrie sang the very song she had been on the road promoting when Keith had overdosed, ''Dear Me.'' She dedicated the song to her late husband's memory. The sad lyrics, coupled with her powerful and emotional delivery, defined the moment. You could have heard a pin drop as she performed. Many, both in the crowd and backstage, were crying. Somehow Lorrie made it through it with more composure than most who had joined her onstage. And she quickly found that she had been right, the support of Opry family, the sound of applause, and the security of the stage was what she really needed to go forward. Besides hadn't Keith worked hard to get someone to recognize her talents? And he too would have wanted her to push on. So, in retrospect, though many would criticize her for it, going on the Opry was probably the best way she could have handled her grief.

As Lorrie buried her husband and tried to explain what had happened to her children, an RCA record plant was printing her first album. Even as she turned out the lights on her life with her husband, even as she admitted to herself that there was nothing she could do or could have done that would have saved him, the spotlight of her own success was growing brighter and brighter. And the only way to keep it growing was to work.

As heartless as it sounded, even as cheap scandal sheets cried out that Morgan was somehow responsible for her husband's death, Lorrie had other commitments that were calling her. There were dates that had been booked. She had a tour in which she was supposed to open for the Statler Brothers. Decisions had to be made about what she could and couldn't do, so that substitutes could be brought in. To their credit, her manager and RCA put no pressure on the recording artist to go back on the road. They told her that it was up to her. They would do whatever she wanted to do. But even without any pressure, the more Lorrie considered what it was she wanted to do, the more she realized what it was she needed to do.

"When I go into one of my songs and hear applause, it's a good feeling," she explained. And she needed those good feelings now worse than ever. As she told everyone who questioned why she would consider immediately going back, "This is what I've worked for, to be recognized and to be respected." It was also the medicine that would bring some kind of healing.

Those who knew the Morgan family knew that the stage held a soothing spirit that Lorrie needed more than she needed anything at this moment. It came as a huge surprise to many when Lorrie almost immediately informed her organization that there would be no time off. They had dates booked and she felt that they should fulfill their contracts as scheduled.

Lorrie had one week off before hitting the road, and it may have been the most difficult week she had ever known. She shared her emotions and feelings about those days with almost everyone in the press over time. Yet she probably cut the deepest and gave the most insight as to what she was going through when she spoke with the Associated Press's Joe Edwards about not only getting on with her life in the days after the funeral, but why she also needed to go back on the road so soon.

"It was difficult just to breathe, to open my eyes," she shared with the writer. "It (going back on the road) was something I felt I had to do to get on with my life. It would have been easy to sit home and mope and cry and stay shut up in a room. But I needed to be around friends, not closed in."

A week into her tour Lorrie told Bruce Miller of the *Sioux City Journal*, "It's what Keith would have wanted." She added in that interview that she needed to get on with her life. Yet as her normal show progressed, as she pushed her material and tried to get the crowd to relax and enjoy her music and stop thinking about her pain, she did allow herself a chance to look back for a brief instant. In front of the more than ten thousand people who had gathered, she sang Keith's biggest hit, "Don't Close Your Eyes." It probably would have been a lot easier on Lorrie if she could have just closed her eyes and made the world go away. What she didn't know, even as "Dear Me" hit the top ten, was that things were only going to get tougher before they got better.

Chapter 9

Lorrie's plate was full just spending time with her children during the crucial days and weeks following her husband's death. Added to this important task was surviving the slings of a tabloid press that seemed intent on blaming her for Keith's untimely passing, while she was working a full schedule of tour dates and trying to come to grips with the fact that she had unexpectedly lost the love of her life. She shouldn't have been subject to so much so quickly, and she certainly shouldn't have had to deal with anything else. But she did.

Keith had no will. Like so many other small details of his life, he simply hadn't taken the time to face that task. Now, in spite of the fact that she and her children had been linked in every major newspaper and magazine in the country for the past three years with Whitley, Lorrie was left with the state in control of a great deal of the couple's estate and having to fight red tape to get her rightful property. Thus, Lorrie was forced to go to court to become the administrator of her husband's estate. Ironically, Whitley, who had spent the last few months of his life being tapped as a superstar and had just become a man who had been so close to cashing in on the big bucks that adoring fans and bookers wanted to cast his way, left an estate that barely totalled $100,000. Off the top of this total came expenses for lawyers and court fees because he had not written a will. As had so often happened in her life, Lorrie was once again trapped in another Catch-22 situation.

Lorrie was quickly faced with the sobering and shocking fact that even if she was the widow of a man who had just scored three straight number one songs, she was still looking at having to work harder than she already was just to pay bills, make car and house payments, and continue to live in the somewhat modest manner she and Keith had managed over the past few months. As if she didn't have enough pressure before, her battles in court had her facing the cold reality of being a sole provider for two small children in a world that was anything but certain really brought the hammer down. Now not only was she in a position to have to do the dates that had already been assigned to her, but she needed more dates to make up for the money that Keith's passing had cost the couple. How was she going to manage it all? Many wondered.

Lorrie hit the road harder than ever, now traveling in Keith's tour bus. This in itself was a bit strange and almost macabre, yet it was the only way that Lorrie could tour in a manner that would allow her to be a full-time mother and a performer. Because Keith's bus could handle the number of people who would be coming with Lorrie, she had to use it. Yet even her rights to use the bus were not fully guaranteed, as the courts had yet to settle who was going to get what in the final settlement of the Whitley's property. And though the bus had been Keith's, for the time being, the state allowed her to use it.

Many widows have to get away from their homes in order to escape the memory of their late spouse. The thoughts of eating at the same table, sleeping in the same bed, sitting in the same chairs as their mates used to occupy is just too much for them. Yet in a strange way, going on the road and getting away from home had just the opposite effect on Lorrie Morgan. As she traveled on his bus from city to city and show to show, Keith was still with her in so many ways. His memory was locked on the bus. His image was in the wings at the shows. Every time she stepped on stage, Lorrie found herself forcing out more feelings and emotions, in large part because her late husband had always asked her to do that and she could still hear him urging her on.

Yet this wasn't the first time Lorrie had experienced

the hand of a dead loved one on her shoulder and in her life. Her father had been with her when she worked after his death. She had felt him and heard his advice even after he was gone. He was still her mentor. And now Keith was her mentor, and she was doing what he had always urged her to do. And it was paying off.

Like never before, Lorrie was singing from the heart, exposing herself and all of her raw emotions to every fan who paid to hear her perform. And she found that the people were responding. Some may have come to see her out of curiosity or even sympathy, but they were leaving knowing that they had just seen a true song stylist—an entertainer, who like George Morgan, had left nothing onstage. Lorrie continued to give it all away night after night and show after show. And even though she might have been using his inspiration to help guide her, Lorrie was building not on her husband's death, as some in the media were claiming, but on what RCA had picked up when they had cut the new album. She was finding herself. She was finding her voice. She was realizing her potential.

As one week turned to two and two to three, Lorrie became a bit more in touch with what had happened to her. The wounds, though open and bleeding, were being acknowledged and she was doing her best to minister to them. During interviews with the press, she often cried a little bit, but she always made it through each session. When things became too tough and questions were too probing, Lorrie acknowledged that there were things she couldn't deal with yet and would move on. When she was with the media, she was honest and didn't try to put a mask on her mourning.

Yet onstage she displayed none of her deep pain to her fans. She put on a happy face for them. She wanted them, especially those who were grieving with her, to know the joy that her music could bring to them too. Night after night, show after show, this move to be positive and up-beat didn't change. The minutes before she went out into the spotlight she might well have been in tears and un-happily drawing on a cigarette, but the second she heard her name she left that part of her life behind her. She reasoned that the fans didn't need to see her bleed, they needed to see her heal. So for them, she attempted to be strong. In truth she would have much preferred caving in.

Her father had once told Lorrie that she always had to be nice. She had taken these words to heart and ever since she had started in this business, she always had been good to her fans. Now they were paying her back for her years of kindness by giving their love back to her. For that reason, and a thousand more, Lorrie couldn't let them know how she really felt, even if it was breaking up her insides. Even now she had to love them even when she felt her heart simply couldn't love anymore. And during this rough time, Lorrie did just that. It was made all the more easier because the fans wanted so to love her back.

Less than a month after her husband had died, Lorrie was back at Fan Fair. For the entire week, she kept a warm smile on her face, posed for pictures with each fan who asked, and tried to steer conversation away from Keith's death. Yet her fan club booth was within the sight line of Keith's. And so no matter where she turned, his image was there reminding her of the numbness and pain that had been with her now for the longest four weeks of her life.

Morgan wanted desperately to look ahead, and working was the best way she knew to do this. Most of the fans seemed to sense her needs and didn't intrude on her personal grief or emotions when they saw her off the stage. Those who did stop simply told her that they were praying for her and moved on. Yet even when she was being surrounded by the images of fans who loved and supported her and a song that had registered in the top ten, there was days when it seemed like she had too much to handle.

She later confessed that there were times when she just wanted to give up, to get out of the business and go and hide. Yet she stuck it out because her kids were there. They needed her and this forced her to go on. Fortunately, she had a role model who was still with her who helped her too.

Lorrie could look back almost two decades and see and honestly appreciate how her own mother had handled her father's sudden death. Even after their long and happy marriage, even after all the good times, even after realizing that her life was going to change dramatically, Anna had refused to give up. She had moved on and had kept her family close. She had done what it took every-day, and she had managed one day at a time.

When Lorrie got really tired and just wanted to go home and lock herself in her room, she also remembered her father's example. When he had been on the road for weeks at a time, when he had driven a thousand miles only stopping for gas and something to eat, even when he hadn't had any sleep in days, he always came home and gave a bit of time to his kids. He was there for them. She knew that no matter how many different ways life was pulling at her, she too had to follow her father's example. She had to make time for her career and her children. Even if that meant giving up any time she had managed to scrape together for herself.

Still, just like her father, the work also pulled her away from some of the most important things in her children's lives. Even though she took them with her when she could, mothering them like a hen did with her chicks, there were times when situations dictated that Morgan and Jesse couldn't go. So Lorrie missed sporting events, programs, and many monumental firsts. It was so difficult for the caring mother to hear about these things through a nanny rather than witnessing them through her own eyes. Mothering over the phone just didn't have the effect that being there in person did either. There was so much joy she couldn't share and so much hurt she couldn't heal. And she felt guilty.

Still even in the midst of working a killer schedule and working out the legal problems with Keith's estate, due in part to her loss and a part to her father's inspiration, Lorrie somehow worked in time to take her kids out to eat, to the park, or to a few movies. Several times that meant even doing interviews from a pay phone in the lobby. Still, Lorrie thought it was worth it. Yet as the dark circles under her eyes seemed to clearly indicate, she was probably spreading herself too thin and pushing too hard.

As Lorrie continued to work a schedule that must have originated in hell, many thought that losing Keith could be heard in her voice. Barry Church, who booked her into the Chattahoochee Mountain Fair, noted that Whitley's passing had added a bit of emotion that now seemed to come out in live shows.

"I think her tragedy had made her a better singer," Church said. Barry then added, "The last thing Keith Whitley told her was that he thought she was headed toward being one of country music's great singers. Right after he died, she had her two biggest hits." Church seemed convinced that not only had Whitley seen what was just ahead for Lorrie, but that he was in large part responsible for it too.

Lorrie appeared to agree with Barry Church when she told Santa Ana, California writer Jim Washburn, "I just feel more emotion in my music now than I ever have. I think a loss like this affects someone's whole life, and it definitely affects the way I sing."

As the summer heated up and Lorrie readied to release her third single of *Leave the Love Light On,* she sensed just how much crowds were responding to her current hit. On stage, "Dear Me" had become the song where she and audience allowed their hearts to beat as one. This story of lost love had turned into a ballad of real mourning. Yet this was also a song that spoke of going on and Lorrie told the fans that it is "my light at the end of the tunnel." But there was still a lot of tunnel to go through and still a lot of work that she was going to be asked to manage before she experienced the full warmth of that light.

In the midst of Lorrie's heavy schedule, RCA asked her to choose Keith's next single. As she listened once again to his hot-selling album, one song struck her as being perfect. She called RCA and told them that she had picked "I Wonder Do You Still Think of Me." Lorrie's instincts were quickly proven right. The Whitley single was released in late June and would eventually climb to number one, becoming Keith fourth straight chart-topping single. While he was no longer around to hear the world respond to his music, he shouldn't have had to wonder if his widow still thought of him. Every time she heard the song on the radio, she cried.

Keith Whitley probably *sold* a song as well as anyone in modern Nashville. When you listened to one of his odes to lost love or heartache, you heard the ragged pain in his voice. Lorrie heard it now more than ever and continued to try to push her own emotions to the edge to reveal her essence through her songs.

"I don't think it's so much what you sing," she explained to those wanting to know why she had suddenly grown so strong as a song stylist. "I think it's how you project it, how you make the audience understand the way you feel it. That's why every song I put in my show has a meaning for me—there's always a reason why it's there."

She had dropped the "Something Special" handle and now called her band, "Slam Band." To strengthen the group's sound, she had also added some of Keith's best players. Sporting this hot live group and having "Dear Me" earn the spot as the number one video in the nation, Lorrie was being noticed now in circles where even Keith Whitley hadn't gotten play. Her video was crossing over to noncountry music video outlets and this was creating new fans who were coming to her concert simply because they had seen the beautiful lady with the haunting voice on television and she had intrigued them. Everyday Lorrie's family of fans was growing at an unparalleled rate.

As has been noted earlier in this chapter and throughout this book, family had always been important to Lorrie, and it was even more important now. Her mother Anna, a woman Lorrie called, "a saint on earth, truly one of the last ladies," had helped her deal with Keith's death at every step. She was there any time her baby needed her. So too were Lorrie's siblings. So it was only natural that when Lorrie was passing through Barberton, Ohio, the community where her father had grown up and found local fame, that she took time out of her killer schedule not to rest, but rather to stop by a nursing home to visit with her ninety-year-old grandmother. While she was there, she got out her guitar and sang, "Candy Kisses." It was the only song that Grandma Morgan really knew, and Lorrie wanted the elderly lady to know that her granddaughter hadn't forgotten it either.

As the August heat gave way to the first hint of the coolness of fall, Morgan finished most of her dates with the Statlers and moved on to a new series of package shows with another long-time country music legend. The rag sheets had had little to say about Lorrie's supposed love life when she had been traveling with the Statlers, but as soon as she landed with Kenny Rogers, the tabloids began having a field day. Less than three months after Whitley's death, patrons at supermarkets were reading about Morgan's supposed affair with Rogers. Lorrie called the reports "sick," but it didn't stop the gossip. Even as "Out of Your Shoes" was beginning to climb the playlists, her name was again being dragged through the mud.

In truth all that Morgan and Rogers had done was go to dinner a couple of times with their bands. They were never alone and while they did visit a great deal, there was no sexual heat generated between the two. Kenny was even married at that time. Yet because Rogers had a reputation (he was known as a "once, twice, three times' lady's man" who had rarely let a wedding ring stand in the way of his fun), Lorrie was being placed in a bad light. It seemed that when the press should have naturally rallied to her side with support, they were having a field day attacking her. Even her friends in the media didn't sugar coat their reports of the singer.

Writers like Jack Hurst, who covered country music a great deal, noted that by late summer Lorrie seemed thin and tired. He thought that she was also smoking more than usual. When he asked her why she was pushing herself so hard, she told the writer that she was working so hard not because she wanted to, but because she was now supporting two children by herself and she needed the money. She also admitted, ''It also helps me keep from sitting around doing nothing except thinking.''

Some felt that her needing the money was just a feeble excuse Lorrie was using to get in front of people and push herself as a product. Many accused her of being guilty of using Keith's death for self-promotion. While it may have seemed that way, this just wasn't the case.

Lorrie was now thirty years old. She knew that this opportunity with RCA was probably the last one she was ever going to receive to be a recording star. With that in mind, she was truly worried about being able to support her children over the long haul. Unless she scored now, she didn't know what kind of future she was going to have. That was why getting out on the road was so important to her. She had known what doing road dates to promote records had meant from her earliest years. The road was where a lot of people made their judgments about you. It was where you earned fans who were loyal. It was where you became something other than ''Lorrie Who'' or ''Keith Whitley's Widow.'' And she knew that even if it might have been creating some press for her career now, this last title would fade quickly too. So in the face of criticism and exhaustion, she kept on moving.

Yet the long bus rides, which should have brought much needed rest, really gave gave her time to think. It allowed her to look back over all she had done and tried to do for Keith. This time she had to think finally allowed her to come to grips with that fact that she couldn't have solved Keith's problem. No matter what the tabloids and the Music City gossip grapevine said, only he could have made that first step toward being sober. And he would have had to have done it one day at a time. No matter how much she wanted him to escape the bottle, he had to want it too. No matter how strong she was for him, he still had to be strong for himself. And now, only after much careful consideration, Lorrie was able to talk about that and to air some thoughts that might just wake up a lot of fans as to how hard she had tried to save Keith.

Of course, the first people who had to know this were her own children.

As much as she could, Lorrie packed up the kids, now eight and two, and took them with her on the road. When her youngest asked about his father, Lorrie explained that "He's in Heaven singing with Jesus." It was the only answer that the mother had, and ultimately she knew that it wouldn't be enough. But when she needed a deeper answer, she would find one. Most importantly, Jesse and Morgan knew that their mother really loved their father and missed him as much as they did.

Meanwhile, even as she was coming to a clear understanding of what had really happened, Lorrie's music was now really on the rise, something that was extremely rare in male and group-driven country music. There is no doubt that opening for groups like the Statlers and Kenny Rogers had probably helped the singer's visibility with the fans. Something else that had played well for a while had been the strength she had shown after her husband's death. But the most important facet that was fueling her career was the mere fact that RCA and producer Barry Beckett had made sure that she was now getting top-notch material and promotion. After all, she could only ride the coattails of a tragedy for a short while, then the talent and material were going to have to take over full-time. By fall, it was obvious that Lorrie was now selling records and earning radio play simply because she and her product were so good.

By the end of September, nine full months into the year, only two new country female acts had broken into Billboard's top twenty during 1989. One was the folk singer Mary Chapin Carpenter, who had two songs leap into the teens. And in truth it was country music's new generation who had put Mary Chapin Carpenter on the charts. The other act who was lighting up playlists was Lorrie. And she had made it because she had strong acceptance across the boards. As Morgan looked forward to being an important part of the Country Music Association's annual October awards show, she could now feel as if she really belonged on the stage with not only the Opry stars, but the current crop of new country music artists as well.

One of the CMA nominations that signaled a bittersweet note for Lorrie belonged to her husband Keith. He had been nominated for Record of the Year. As she sat in the audience and listened to the nominees' names clicked off, Lorrie couldn't help but pray that her son's father would finally be chosen a winner. When they called Keith's name, she shook her head and moved confidently toward the stage.

Keith Whitley's single "I'm No Stranger to the Rain," deserved to be recognized by the CMA as the Single of the Year. It was one of the most haunting, beautiful ballads in the history of country music and Whitley had sung the heck out of it. Yet as wonderful as the song was, the few seconds where Lorrie accepted the award for the late star was one of the most touching and emotional of any in the history of the awards show and they rivaled the emotion that her late husband had shown in his song.

Lorrie didn't make a big deal of her speech. She refused to allow this moment to become a sad one. Showing the inner strength that had guided her through the last half year, she thanked those responsible for the song and then acknowledged the greatness of Keith Whitley's talent. Her job done, she elegantly walked off the stage to a thunderous hand of applause. Yet she would soon return to her seat as this award was not to be the only reason Lorrie had shown up for the show.

Later in the evening, Morgan was somewhat disappointed but not surprised when she didn't win the award for Video of the Year. Losing that award to Hank Williams, Jr. and Hank Williams, Sr. for "There's a Tear in My Beer" didn't hit her nearly as hard as watching her father passed over for the Country Music Hall of Fame. Lorrie had no problems with Hank Thompson making the Hall, she just felt that they should have made room for George Morgan too. The longer the years from the time of his death, the more she was worried that the CMA might just forget the man who had made "Candy Kisses" one of the nation's most beloved songs. This fear was evident when Lorrie met the press after the closing of the show.

Morgan told Ellis Widner of the *Tulsa Tribune*, "I am glad I could bring one home for Keith. I wish I could have brought one home for Dad too."

Yet her disappointment didn't take Lorrie's focus away from capitalizing on the fact that a lot of people who made decisions now knew who she was. As a part of Country Music Week in Nashville, she got out and met the movers and shakers. And during the week, Lorrie took time out to impress bookers at the annual CMA talent showcase. Her strong-stage presence knocked a number of these talent buyers out of their seats. They were looking at the future of this business, and many of them now realized they were seeing a big part of that future when they were watching Lorrie work. As the buyers left her showcase, Morgan felt confident that her dates would be improving as she looked into the next decade.

Maybe because she had worked through so much so quickly, after the show she also began to speak out more. For the first time in public, Lorrie was using the constant interest the press had developed in her career, to get a few things off her chest. Lorrie was finally beginning to talk about the pain of alcohol abuse on not just those who were suffering with the disease, but their families as well. As Lorrie was able to look at her years with Keith with the perspective only the passing of time could bring, she was seeing alcoholism as more than just his problem and something that she had to live with. She now saw it in the lives of thousands of people who came to her shows, bought her products, and talked with her at her autograph sessions. She became so aware of just how much this type of abuse effected the entire nation, that she took time out of her busy schedule and traveled to the Ocean Opry Concert Theater in Panama City, Florida to do two shows that would benefit organizations involved in treating drug and alcohol abuse. This benefit would begin a pattern of service and fund-raising that would continue to grow for years. As if she wasn't busy enough with just her career and her family, now she had a cause she felt that she had to devote a great deal of time to also. She was bound and determined to save others from a death like Keith's.

This move was probably as good a therapy for Morgan as getting right back to work right after she had buried her husband. Now when she talked about Keith, she was fully able to confront both the negative and the positive sides of his life. She was able to talk about all the other times she had almost lost him. She was able to tell just how booze had cheated him out of so much time with his kids and her. Yet even as she acknowledged that Keith Whitley had some very dark moments in his life, and even as she touched upon the alcohol and the problems it created, she would tell reporters and the public, "I was lucky to have had that love for three years." She never referred to her life with him as ever having been a living hell. Even though she had so many opportunities to take the low road, paint Keith in such as way as to make herself look like a saint, she never did.

In Lorrie's mind, even after six months, Keith was still her husband. Even though he was gone and wasn't coming back, he was still with her. She admitted to the press and friends that she couldn't even imagine being with another man. This made the tabloid stories of her romances seem so obscene and ridiculous. She was just not ready to commit to anything other than a husband who had left her far too soon.

It may have been just because the shock was wearing off, but she now began to fully realize just what Keith's death had cost the singer himself. He didn't get to see the public fully embrace his music. "I Wonder Do You Think of Me" went to the top, and "It Ain't Nothing," which had been released after the CMA show, was racing up the charts too. Keith's album was being snapped up so fast that the RCA presses were working overtime just to keep up with demand. And yet sadly, there just wouldn't be much else left for the fans to enjoy.

The fact that the world had just seemingly discovered Keith Whitley bothered her too. She told Jack Hurst that she wanted to "cuss the world out," because it happened too late. She thought that if the fans had really caught on to how good he was sooner, then it might have saved him. Morgan fretted that her late husband never did get to really absorb the love that the crowds now had for his music. If he had, then that might have given him the strength to face his own insecurities. In truth, this rising anger that was now at times revealing itself, probably reflected Lorrie's own feelings of loss and her own fatigue from going so strong for such a long period of time, more than it did her true emotions. She seemed to believe, at that moment when it really had mattered most, people inside and outside the business had taken her father and husband for granted. They didn't give them their due. And now she wanted them both to be recognized so very badly.

Morgan, who had to have so many jumbled emotions running through her system during this time, also may have been feeling a bit guilty too. Her sudden success, after years of going nowhere, was due in no small part to two men who couldn't be there to enjoy these good times with her.

She told the *Tulsa Tribune* as she readied herself to do a show with Ricky Skaggs, "It does feel good to see my career doing something. I wondered if it would ever happen. I would see all these talented new women come to town, getting recording deals. I had been here all of my life and wasn't getting anywhere." Yet she also spent time bemoaning the fact that she wished Keith and her father could have experienced her success too.

So by a cruel twist of fate, even though she was one of the most successful acts in country music, there was still a pall surrounding the young woman. Maybe in part because she did talk about it so much, Lorrie was often still written about and known more as the daughter of a dead star and the widow of a dead star than she was a star in her own right. She did nothing to escape this label when she always worked George Morgan and Keith Whitley songs into her act.

Lorrie told Loretta Macias of the San Angelo, Texas, *Standard-Times*, "I'm proud of those two factors. Being

George Morgan's daughter is very special. When he died, he had a lot of fans who were devastated. For them to still be able to see a part of him in me is gratifying.'' She went on to say that being Keith Whitley's wife was the greatest title she knew. And she added, ''I will never love anyone like I love him.''

By December, Lorrie was not only facing her first Christmas as a widow, but as a single mother of two. It had to have helped that ''Out of Your Shoes'' had earned the number one mark in most parts of the nation (number two on the Billboard lists). This seemed to prove that Lorrie had worked her way through the bad times. She had come out on top. But as she told friends, she now realized that her late husband had worked too much and too hard, and now she was guilty of the same thing. When she recalled her exhaustive travels with George Jones, she knew this high price simply wasn't worth it. She wasn't going to give the business 300 days a year. If that is what it took to catch Reba, then she would just follow along behind. She was going to make sure that she had time to enjoy life. Heaven knows, as she had already discovered through the deaths of her father and husband, no one knew just how much life they ever had left to enjoy.

Chapter 10

Lorrie began the year by setting a goal of doing something that her father had never accomplished, winning a Country Music Association award. This lofty ambition was one that her record label also seemed set on reaching too. But with Reba McEntire's career still seemingly spiraling upward at the speed of light, many within the profession questioned if anyone would ever be anything but a pretender as long as the Oklahoma redhead remained focused. With the addition of several new female acts to record labels, the odds against Morgan's reaching her goal seemed long indeed.

Yet as driven as Reba was, Lorrie was also driven to excel with a sound that could be bested by no other female artist. Much like another second generation up and comer, Pam Tillis, Morgan believed that to really make it to the top and stay there in today's competitive market, a singer had to produce albums that were filled with quality product. McEntire had done this for the past five years and had generated sales once reserved for only the top male stars. Long-playing disks had to now be carefully thought out. Each song was important. Understanding the importance of this and with thoughts of platinum dancing in her head, Lorrie had been listening to tapes for her second RCA album for months. She was determined not to fall into a sophomore jinx syndrome.

Though almost everyone was excited by the singer's work ethic and determination, many thought that Lorrie's immersing herself in every facet of her recording career was also a way to escape some of the elements of her personal life with which she simply didn't want to have deal. While she might have said she was working toward goals, they believed that she had been working hard to avoid lingering grief. If this was the case, then this hard work was nothing more than an extension of the therapy she had used when she had appeared on the Opry stage the day after Keith's funeral. Country music was a source of healing and understanding for Morgan, and when she needed to be baptized in this mixture of work and medicine, she used her career to make it all possible. If it healed her and propelled her toward her goals, then all the better.

During the first weeks of January it was time to record again. Lorrie waltzed into the studio fully prepared and put the first six songs down. In a move that signaled just how much the artist had grown, Morgan would then take a break to listen to even more new material and get a new spin on her project. It would be a couple of months before she would come back into the studio and add the four cuts that would complete her newest LP. Yet the singer wasn't idle during this time of continuing research. There was too much to do to take a much-needed rest.

Coming off the series of hits she had produced during the last year of the eighties, Lorrie was obviously one of the focal points of the country music press. With the sexy, yet tragic Morgan, scribes always had a good source for an interesting feature. Yet with more and more people calling and more and more bookers demanding that the singer work their venue, as well as dealing with her role as a mother of two young children, Lorrie began to find that she had less and less time to give the press. The star who had once been so available was now sometimes unavailable. And when she did talk, she didn't sugarcoat anything. She was almost always direct, straightforward, and honest. This interviewing style often led to many misusing Morgan's quotes. When this began to happen more and more, when the tabloid press hovered constantly like vultures, Lorrie backed off and became more careful, trusting only those who had dealt fairly with her in the past. And for the first time in her career, it seemed that Lorrie was hard for the press to pin down.

This new Lorrie, the young woman who was emerging

as a superstar, therefore seemed different to many. And she was. She was more mature, wiser, and geared more toward protecting her children and her private life. She also was even more vocal about making sure that she had time for herself and the people who needed her most. In the studio she loudly stated her opinions. Upon seeing this new, more confident attitude, many in the media and many within the music business begin call her stuck-up and snobby. The word "bitch" was now often tossed around both in articles and in the stage gossip. Those who had known Lorrie for years knew better than to think of her this way, but a host of others were buying into this presentation of the hot country singer.

"Lorrie is really shy," confirmed country music entertainer Louise Mandrell. "She is quiet and reserved until you get to know her." Far from being a bitch, Mandrell considered Morgan honest and direct, a woman who was strong enough to stand up for things she believed in, but had a heart big enough to always reach out to those about whom she cared.

By and large Mandrell's assessment of Morgan was probably right, yet as much as Lorrie had been through, it was little wonder that the singer didn't open up as quickly as many others who were seen as up-and-comers. The two men whom she had loved most had been snatched from her when she had needed both of them the most. She had lost so much, felt so much pain, and yet still she had managed to go on. And if all the heartache had to take a toll by making her withdraw a bit, then it seemed a small price for the media to pay. It certainly didn't give them a right to label her as something she really wasn't and make accusations about her life that had no basis in truth. Yet in the nineties, with the tabloid mentality of so many of the hot magazines and reporters beginning in the dirt, this seemed to be what drove newsstand sales.

At the Opry, her home away from home, Lorrie could escape the torments of the gossipmongers and the demands of the road. Here, on country music's most hallowed stage, she would often show up on nights when she wasn't working just to sit in the wings and visit with her oldest friends. Spending time with folks like Connie Smith, whom Morgan had known and trusted for years, was like a breath of fresh air. And with Connie and her other stage buddies, the very ones who had watched her grow up, Lorrie had no fronts, she didn't have to carefully guard her emotions or how she phrased her words, and she could depend upon this group keeping her deepest emotions and thoughts to themselves. They were family.

Another group Lorrie remained basically open to was her fans. Those fans, who now had a tougher time getting to her because of the demands of her fame, still loved her. For many she was the most important thing in their lives. Most couldn't name just one favorite Lorrie Morgan song, they liked them all. So in a very real sense, at the fan level Lorrie was evoking loyalty and love like no recent female artist with the exception of Reba. The press may have changed and the business may have evolved, but the real country music fans were pretty much like they always had been. And this small blonde was a throwback to a time when the artist and fan had a special relationship with each other that was more than business—it was personal. Lorrie's father would have been proud to see how his daughter cared for the men and women who paid for the ride.

Most of the folks who bought tickets to watch Lorrie work were just simple people from small homes who came out to the big arenas. These fans almost always told her that they loved her and were praying for her. They remembered her birthday and her children's names. They often asked about her mother. Maybe that was why Lorrie knew that these common people would understand when she would talk about some things and leave other things buried under a full range of contradictory emotions. The fans had suffered through many hard times in their own lives and knew that there were times when there were no words that could be said. Unlike so many in the press, they accepted this and looked for no hidden agendas behind every sigh or every action. Whatever

Lorrie gave them was enough, and night after night, she gave a great deal.

So as country music had become more and more of a big business where most stars treated their fans more like customers than friends, Morgan had tried to remain true to her father's ideals and standards. Lorrie had reached out to the fans with her heart and, not surprisingly, they gave freely back to her from theirs. And perhaps because of this mutual respect and love, the singer also now gave back a bit more than just a great show and good music too. When she got the chance she went to high school and college kids, speaking about the problems that alcohol and drinking could create in their lives. And they usually listened because even the kids who really didn't know who she was sensed that Lorrie was sincere and really cared about them.

"That's something I feel like I can contribute to young kids who are idolizing country music singers," Morgan told the press. "(I can) let them know we don't all do drugs, and we're normal like anybody else and want good things from life."

A 1990 *Country Music Magazine* article described Morgan as "worldly wise, slightly cynical survivor of the graduate school of hard knocks." In the free-wheeling article written by Bob Allen, Morgan opened up fully to the writer and talked to him like she did the students and fans with whom she visited. She spoke about how strongly she was against alcohol and drugs. She talked of it killing those who were under too much stress or worked too hard. She talked about how Keith was at the end of his rope when he died. She also admitted that she was worn out and at the end of hers too right now.

There was little wonder that she was at the end of her rope. Not only was her career growing faster than even she could comprehend, but she simply couldn't seem to bury her late husband. Not only did the press want to keep the story alive, but the courts did too. Lorrie was still spending a good portion of what was supposed to be her free time, not to mention a lot of her money, fighting with the state to get Keith's estate in order. Everything that wasn't in her name was contested. She had to battle to get something as simple as a car title that had been in both of their names transferred over to her so that she could sell it. There were times when it would have seemed a great deal easier just to throw up her hands and tell Tennessee that they could have it all. Yet that would not have been fair to Lorrie's children. And so the legal war dragged on.

So even as "Five Minutes," the song which Pam Tillis had once recorded but had not become a hit single during its first go-around, was climbing the charts, on its way to number one, many of Lorrie's friends were still concerned that Morgan was simply not as happy as she should have been. Her dreams were coming true. She was a star, but there seemed to be so little joy in her heart. The dark circles under her eyes, the softness in her greetings, this was not the Lorrie that they had known up until a year ago.

Even Morgan recognized that there was an element in her that was different. She told Don Rhodes in his *Atlanta Chronicle* "Ramblin' Rhodes" column, "I'm not basically a sad person . . . I'm dealing with being both a mommy and daddy the best way I can, and it's hard to get over the loss of a good man. It is just going to take a while for my life to get back on a happy-go-lucky type of thing again."

As Lorrie hit the road and worked with a variety of different acts, she began to notice something that few others seemed to note. And what she observed gave her a source of satisfaction. Morgan had known the ins and outs of country music for all of her more than three decades, and now something behind the scenes was different. And maybe it had something to do with Keith too! After the show band members and entertainers didn't seem to want to go out and party with each other. A Coke and a meal was now often taking the place of a six pack and a poker game.

Lorrie told the *LA Times,* "I definitely think that the hard-living attitude of country music is changing. I just hate that it is stopping a little too late for Keith.'' She went on to spell out in the interview that the party atmosphere of booze and hard living that were once an ''important'' and accepted part of road life now seemed to be a part of the past. Back then drinking was the way that people thought they had to act in order to be cool, she conceded. Now it was different. She added, ''I think now you're not going to happen any more if you're that way. There's too many talented people that are straight.''

Just like an alcoholic had to take one step at a time in a program to get his or her life cleaned up, Lorrie was understanding that she was having to work through the grieving process very slowly too. And just about the time she had it licked, it seemed that something else came back to remind her of the hole in her life caused by Keith's tragic death.

To her friends and family Lorrie credited her faith with taking her on her step-by-step journey. During this period she would not go on stage until she asked Jesus to give her a good show. As she walked out to meet her fans, she also used her hand to make the sign of the cross.

In a sense what would seem radical to many fundamentalist Christians was not this ''normal'' leaning on the arms of Jesus, what was strange to many was that Lorrie also still felt Keith with her during every one of her shows. To Lorrie it really seemed as if her late husband was there watching over her and giving her the strength of his soul. In a theological sense this seemed to reveal that the singer had a unique mix of New Age and Christian thinking, but for Lorrie there was no conflict. She was sure that her faith and Keith were pulling her through night after night. And because of this faith, Lorrie had grown to the point where success wasn't as important to her as many had believed it was in the months after Whitley's passing. This was a part of the step-by-step healing process.

Carl Hoover of the *Waco Tribune-Herald* got Lorrie to reveal that when he probed her feelings about her quick rise to the top. Morgan explained to Hoover that the success she had seen had been the ''light at the end of the tunnel.'' Yet in an even more intimate bit of wisdom she added, ''A career can't hold you at night, and it can't comfort you.'' So even while she was rising up, she also had to face lonely days of coming down.

Lorrie might have held to her faith in God and worked like the devil to deal with her loss, but she had discovered that the pain and loneliness were still there even in the midst of all the adulation and success. The facts were that faith and the jingle of the cash register couldn't make these emotions go away either. Success was not easy, it was hard. Yet losing a loved one was infinitely harder.

Lorrie told Hoover, ''I'd like to earn enough money to retire at an early age.'' It seemed that Morgan knew now, even more than she had when she had worked with George Jones, that there was more to life than the road. It might have even been tempting to walk away from it all. And even as she came to grips with this, the woman whom *People* magazine was calling the ''no-frills Dolly Parton,'' was facing another year of living on the concrete ribbon between dates. And everyone knew that she wouldn't quit.

In late May, RCA threw a party for the singer at the Ryman Auditorium. There Lorrie was presented her first Gold record by Opry stage manager Hal Durham and RCA senior vice president Joe Galante. Lorrie told those gathered, ''I feel fortunate to have been given a lot of chances to prove my ability as a person and as a singer. There'll be mistakes along the way, I'm sure, but with people like you behind me we'll pick up the pieces and go forth once more.''

Lorrie then gave her mother a gold plaque for ''having traveled thousands of miles with me just to make sure I'd get there safe.'' Just like Morgan refused to forget the fans, she wasn't going to forget the woman who had backed her when few others had given her a chance.

The gold certification came just ten months after *Leave the Light On*'s release, thus allowing Lorrie to join K. T. Oslin's *80's Ladies* and Anne Murray's *Snowbird,* as the only debut albums by female country artists to go gold. Ironically, the presentation also came almost exactly a year since the day that Lorrie had suffered the most crushing loss of her life. Yet there was no time for Morgan to consider her loss or savor her victory, she had too many dates to work to give more than a moments thought to much of anything.

The Sesser Opry House in Kentucky, which the year before had sold 100 tickets for Lorrie's show, invited her back and was rewarded with two sold-out performances. Now there were 1,300 on hand for her hour-long seventeen-song set. Yet this show was a small show now.

For Lorrie, who only a few years before thought that 1,000 people was a throng, with her records climbing the charts now usually more than 10,000—many of whom had come out just for her—was the norm. It had to be satisfying to also now get notes from old friends who had once written her off as a wannabe. The singer loved the fact that a host of former school mates who used to make fun of her for singing country music and hanging out at the Opry were now calling for tickets to her shows. Yet rather than write them off, as most people would have and they had her two decades before, Lorrie returned their calls and sent them tickets.

Her dates were getting better as her fame was on the upswing. She was working solo at the big venues such as Tyler Texas's Oil Palace. Now there were fewer clubs and fairs and a lot more arenas. Her show generally began with a hot up-tempo number such as Charlie Rich's "Lonely Weekends," then a quick switch into her own hits like "Out of Your Shoes," "Dear Me," "He Talks to Me," and " 'Till a Tear Becomes a Rose," and finally onto her father's "Candy Kisses." Working Slam Band into a frenzy, she now often belted out some old rock and roll before usually closing with "Faithfully," a song originally released by Journey. With sexy, silky outfits and plenty of audience chatter, she constantly earned great reviews and standing ovations.

In April, Morgan had released the final single off her incredibly successful *Leave the Light On* album. "He Talks to Me" spoke to millions of fans in a big way too. The single was a rare bird in the world of country music.

It was the fifth release off Lorrie's debut album. Five releases off one LP was simply unheard of in Music City. Usually there just wasn't that much good stuff to ship. Yet this album held a lot of gold. Racing to the top ten, the single peaked at number four by early summer.

Lorrie's tremendous popularity really became evident when she was nominated for the TNN/Music City News Female Vocalist of the Year, Star of Tomorrow, and Video of the Year ('Dear Me') awards. While she wouldn't win any of them, the nominations did give her a bit more of the needed status to impress the CMA. No longer was she daddy's little girl in anyone's eyes, she was a star. And with the fans' votes she was still on her way up.

The single "Till a Tear Becomes a Tear" marked a unique place in Lorrie's career. She had once recorded a duet with her late father, now she did the same thing with her late husband. The single, haunting and sad, was released in July and managed a ride to number thirteen. The irony of peaking at that, the unluckiest of numbers, was not lost on many in the Whitley/Morgan camp. Even in the midst of great success, there were still signs of the old hard luck.

Lorrie's fashion model looks, now topped with an easy-to-maintain, close-cropped hairdo (some called it punk), had already graced countless magazines by mid-summer. And she had also appeared on the all-important NBC's *Tonight Show*. The show's host, Jay Leno, and Lorrie traded quips as if they were old friends. It was obvious that not only Leno, but his fans got into Lorrie in a big way. L.A. seemed to want to see more of Morgan, and with the daring gowns she was sporting, there wasn't much left for them to see. Yet the folks on the West Coast weren't alone in registering their approval.

Norfolk, Virginia reviewer Frank Roberts caught Lorrie with Alabama and Clint Black and wondered why the hot star wasn't even hotter. Roberts wrote, "She had good audience rapport, chatting a lot, and has a big, beautiful country voice." And she was never satisfied, even when the reviews were this good. She kept pushing to improve the show each night.

For reasons which she didn't share with fans or the press, by mid-year Lorrie was beginning her package with the Amy Grant contemporary Christian hit, "Love of Another Kind." Yet in a stage production that seemed centered on all kinds of love, including that between a star and her fans, why shouldn't Morgan want to present her own faith in a very subtle way. This kind of Christian love was a great set-up for her to talk about another kind of love that was still with her too.

One of the most touching moments during each of her 1990 shows was when she used taped music to duet with Keith on " 'Til a Tear Becomes a Rose." The controlled emotion and powerful song styling she displayed on this, as well as numbers like "Dear Me," had reviewers beginning to compare her to Tammy Wynette and Reba McEntire. And it had fans crying.

Writing for the *Tulsa World,* John Wooley noted, "It was a show that was unabashedly country in the old sense, even though everything about the performance, from Morgan's hairstyle to the electronic keyboards, was state of the art." He also added, "A lot of entertainers know how to work a crowd, but after seeing Lorrie Morgan at Tulsa City Limits Thursday night, I'd put her up against any of them." Scores of other critics, even those who had once thought of her as just a novelty act, were now falling in love with almost everything she did.

As the hits kept coming in, Lorrie allowed herself to realize that she really was on the verge of making the big time. "I've paid a lot of dues, learned a lot, seen people come and go," she told several reporters. "I think I'm ready for success. I guess this is the big final test when you have your exams."

As she earned the praises of the industry, Lorrie shared with friends that she would gladly trade the success she had dreamed of almost all of her life to have simply had more time with Keith. "But it's not my decision to make," she lamented even as she openly admitted to being bitter and confused and wondering out loud why God would put this on her.

Yet as the days rushed by and the time between her husband's life and death passed, Lorrie did begin to see more and more positive things that had come out of the nightmare. She told Lynn Rollings of the *Montgomery Alabama Journal*, "I could have probably lived the rest of my life dependent on someone else—dependent on Keith. But his death made me grow up."

And she didn't stop this direction of thinking with just the Rollings interview, Lorrie constantly spoke to other reporters of what she had gone through as a maturing experience. She even noted that she saw her performance and music as the therapy that allowed her to survive. Those who had watched her put herself through the hellish schedule of the last year knew that the singer was right on in her assessments.

As *Leave the Light On* continued to rack up huge sales, Lorrie found herself jetting past one of most publicized albums released by one of the most highly visible self-promoters in the industry. The album was *White Limozeen* by Dolly Parton. It seemed that one blonde had given way to another. At least in this case Morgan's product was even bigger and more visible than Parton's. In country music this was saying a great deal! Few women could emerge from Dolly's shadow.

Yet even as Lorrie's name was placed on the Fargo Walk Of Fame and she had left her hand prints in cement beside such luminaries as Chet Atkins, Joan Jett, Stevie Ray Vaughan, Cloris Leachman, Gregory Hines, and Dr. Norman Vincent Peale, she knew that this meant nothing without the recognition that went with an awards show in October. And as the summer gave way to the fall, she couldn't help but wonder if she would meet her most important goal or have to start all over again next year.

In the 1990 CMA show Reba McEntire sat still as the winner of the Female Vocalist Award was announced. Unfortunately, so did Lorrie. Kathy Mattea walked away with the honor for the second year in a row. While McEntire would largely be left out of the awards, Morgan would finally get to accept one of the statues for herself. The Country Music Association recognized her and Keith Whitley for vocal event of the year with " 'Till a Tear Becomes a Rose.''

In a sense, winning the award may have brought Lorrie and Keith together for another time, but it also may have allowed Morgan to come to grips with his passing too. She had helped him to hit the spotlight a final time, just as he had helped her get into the spotlight in a big way a few years before. Now it was time to put all the ghosts to rest and move on.

By the end of the year, Lorrie was dating again. One of the men on her arm was veteran country star Johnny Rodriguez. When the two performed together in San Antonio for New Years, reporters questioned their relationship. Lorrie simply said that Johnny was a true gentleman. Rodriguez went a bit further, "Yes, Lorrie and I are dating and she told me it's OK to say I'm her boyfriend and she's my girlfriend." Morgan had finally moved on. She was letting herself enjoy life again and discovering that she had quite a life to enjoy too!

In just two years with RCA, Lorrie had equalled the chart and sales success that it had taken her father almost three decades to reach. This showed not only how far the singer had come, but how much the industry had grown. In George's day, a hit might sell 30,000 copies. Now a hit album would turn millions. In her father's day, few big-time publications noticed country music, now *Playboy* was calling and offering big bucks to country music's hottest sex symbol. The magazine wanted her to share her buxom figure with the world. They saw her as a ticket for millions in newsstand sales. Even as she ignored Hugh Hefner's call, the mere thought that she was now considered figuratively and literally so hot had to have pleased Morgan. Yet there was still much to be done to achieve the kind of lasting fame that would allow her to soon escape the horrid pace that had controlled her life over the last eighteen months.

Lorrie, whose reputation for selling product was based entirely on one project, realized that the pressure was on to produce like results during the second release. Otherwise she was simply going to be another act who blazed for an instant before returning to the "where are they now" circles. And as long as she had an influence in her career, she wasn't going to let it happen either.

Chapter 11

As 1991 began, it seemed that almost everyone wanted to visit with Lorrie. The phone was ringing off the wall with old friends, family, and members of the media looking for the CMA's latest winner. And with that award, the fully booked tour schedule, a new album about to be released and sales still soaring for her debut RCA LP, life seemed to be about as good as it could get. Yet early in the year, as she ate chicken at Prince's, a Nashville restaurant that served her favorite hot, spiced fried variety of bird, she told a country music reporter that she wondered what it would have been like if Keith hadn't died. And as she considered the demands that were being made daily on her own life, she also wondered if the price she was currently paying for fame was too high.

As she ate, Lorrie explained to Neil Pond of *Country America*, "Years ago, I could have killed somebody and not gotten into the *Enquirer*. Now, all of a sudden, if I turn around wrong, it gets written about." Yet facts were facts, and even if the tabloids hadn't "made up" stories to sell extra newsstand issues, Lorrie was still making news. In some cases she *was* news!

Morgan's *Leave the Light On* was now assured platinum status. This was almost unheard of for a Music City female artist. Long ago the LP had passed double gold. Five hit singles off the project labeled her as a special kind of performer with a special kind of talent. Even Reba hadn't accomplished that! And her road shows were winning great reviews too. The fact was that as a singer she was being constantly compared to Tammy Wynette, a woman who had produced so many classic recordings that she had cracked the top twenty-five all-time chart list.

On the road the scribes likened her to Barbara Mandrell. Few critics had ever dared to compare other acts to Barbara. Her show was so electric, so entertaining, so exciting, that Mandrell's little sister Louise might have just been the only one to have surpassed it. Yet now Morgan had matured as a performer to the point where she was being placed in that category too. So even if their personal life hadn't been so doggone interesting, Lorrie would have still been newsworthy. People would have still wanted to write about her.

Yet even though more and more people wanted to know more and more about every facet of her being, by and large Morgan had become more and more tight-lipped about her personal life. She had been burned far too often in the past. Yet even though she had placed a growing portion of her personal life off the record, as she began to be offered more new opportunities professionally, she didn't mind visiting about a project that had taken almost one year in the making—her new album.

From the moment she mentioned the title, it was easy to see that the singer was very excited about *Something in Red.* From first cut to last, she actually believed that this release would be her best work yet. For a woman who had issued five hit singles from her last project, this was saying something! How in the world, many wondered, could she top what she had done on her initial run from the blocks?

As she met with friends and members of the press, Morgan proudly talked about going over the top on the new project. She explained that she had had to go that extra mile because of how difficult it was going be to follow the success of the first album. She therefore wanted every single to be perfect and every song to be as strong as any release. In other words, she thought that this album had ten single possibilities, not just five!

Morgan had something else in mind when she produced a product with so much care and quality. With her status as a hitmaker assured, Lorrie knew that she was now going to be compared to *herself* and not Tammy, Dolly, Reba, or Barbara. And these new comparisons would be even harder to measure up to than those she had received when the industry had labeled her simply as "George Morgan's daughter." Yet because she was the daughter of a country music star, she also knew that if she didn't produce a winner with her second release, then she would probably be marked down as a loser forever. That was the nature of this business. Country music was full of one-hit or one-year artists who simply faded away and were never heard from again. Lorrie didn't want to become a name on this list, and as she worked on this album, she decided that to insure it didn't happen, she would take more control. In doing this she set incredibly high standards to live up to also. Her challenge was to top Lorrie Morgan. And many, even at RCA, didn't know how she was going to do this.

One of the concerns that the music community seemed to have was that the album had taken a long time to put together. In late 1989 when RCA had put the word out that Lorrie needed new material for an album, about the only thing they received was "dying" songs. Just when Morgan seemed ready to leave the past behind, every writer in town wanted to revisit it. It seemed that the material was more downbeat than upbeat, and Lorrie didn't want to deal with that anymore. She didn't want to sound like a widow, she wanted to put out the kind of product that folks like Reba McEntire did—solid, first-class songs that revolved around a wide variety of themes and styles. That need for a new kind of material was the reason that the singer had spent so long working on the album, and with it had then taken even longer to get it right in the studio.

One of the songs on the new project had been a big surprise, even to Lorrie. When in the midst of putting together material for *Something in Red,* Morgan had been booked from Nashville to Los Angeles on a commercial flight. When she sat down, she couldn't help but note that Dolly Parton was in the seat next to her. Lorrie wouldn't have even considered approaching the buxom legend with the request to sing with her, and yet the opportunity to do so seemed almost to fly into her lap. Yet, showing a great deal of restraint and class, Lorrie didn't jump on the opportunity. Rather, the two performers spent the whole flight talking about everything else. Then, in the midst of their conversation about family, Parton mentioned that it would be great for them to cut a song together. Lorrie thought that Dolly was just flattering the younger singer, didn't take Parton seriously, but still showed the good sense to agree. This duet talk might have gone no farther, but fate was about to step in again.

Two days later, when both of them were headed back to Nashville, Parton and Morgan again found themselves sitting together. Dolly again brought the idea of recording together up, and pointblank informed Lorrie that she would write something for them. Busy with her own schedule, Morgan thanked Parton as they parted in Music City and figured that the duet concept would die right there. She would soon find out that Dolly was really serious.

A few weeks later Dolly had put something together, recording a rough of the composition, and began looking for Lorrie. The superstar tracked Morgan down on the road in Florida. Dolly informed Morgan that the song was a go and express-delivered a surprised Lorrie a demo. From the first playing, Lorrie fell in love with it.

With both singers now assured that they wanted to do something, they began to look for a time to meet in the studio. This was far from an easy mission. It took some planning and rearranging, but within weeks the labelmates were laying down the tracks on the new song that Dolly had penned for the occasion. For Lorrie it was a big thrill, but for Dolly it was a good career move. Parton knew that this recording represented a chance for her to mix with some of the hot new country sounds that were beating her at the check-out counters and on the playlists. It might just give her slightly sagging career a bit of a boost. As Dolly had helped pave the way for Lorrie, the younger singer didn't mind in the least giving Parton a lift.

Yet it wasn't the joining with Dolly, nor was it the release of the album's first single, "We Both Walk," which would hit number three on the charts, that was to define the new project. There was one song, a haunting, lyrical ride into the story of a woman's life, that would establish this album as one of the most unique and special in the long history of country music.

"I was pitched that song by Barry Beckett," Lorrie explained, "who was originally supposed to coproduce the album. I hated it. I listened to the first verse and I passed on it."

Because of conflicts, Barry Beckett had to work in other areas and couldn't continue with the project. RCA then assigned Richard Landis to produce Lorrie's second record. Landis stepped in, brought a few ideas with him, and pitched Morgan "Something in Red" again. Richard had been unaware of Lorrie's feelings about the song, but even if he had know them, he loved this composition so much, he probably would have pitched it anyway. Lorrie still had bad vibes about the number, but decided that she had better go back and listen to the whole song before making her final judgment. If everyone loved it, she thought, then it deserved a second chance.

Angela Kaset had written this classic of the story of a woman who sees the stages of her life through the clothes she wore. And as the song's powerful lyrics began to echo in Lorrie's head, she saw their potential too, especially when coupled to her own torchy ballad style. Putting her reservations aside, she accepted the song that would become one of her signature pieces. "Something In Red" most assuredly was the crowning note on the project that had to better *Leave the Light On.* Thanks largely to that song, the album was better too!

As the initial reviews began to come in, *Something in Red* immediately appeared to be a real winner. It might have been almost two years in the making, but the critics agreed that it was worth the wait.

Miami Herald's Mario Tarradell wrote, "(*Something*

In Red) firmly establishes her as a country vocalist with a torch. Her voice is smooth, silky, and filled with raw emotion. . . . The title cut is a showpiece.''

People magazine added, ''She's a major-league country performer.''

Music critic Tad Richards noted, ''Lorrie Morgan comes into her own this time, hot and sexy and torchy and southern, wailing over a beat, purring over a sinuous guitar or sobbing over strings. She runs her voice across a range of emotions, slighting none of them.'' Yet this was only the beginning of the good news. As the weeks passed and the review copies were played, the glowing tributes kept rolling in.

Jim Abbott, of the *Orlando Sentinel* (not the California Angels), waxed, ''If *Something In Red* is any indication, Morgan won't have to worry about living in Keith Whitley's shadow for much longer. She'll be busy casting one of her own.''

Yet even as the press began to quit asking the Whitley questions, Lorrie had discovered that getting over Keith was not getting any easier. As her children grew older and wanted to know more about him, they wanted to listen to his music and watch his videos. So even if the tabloids had backed off, even if the rumor mill was no longer claiming that Morgan had had Whitley killed, all around the singer's home were baskets filled with memories of her late husband. And these reminders called her back to just how much of her life, as well as his, was wasted when he drank himself to death.

Yet in the light of all the bad stuff and the doubts, she indicated to her friends and her children that her faith has remained strong. She hung onto the beliefs of her own mother that God had a reason in everything that happens. Yet even as she pushed these bittersweet words from her mouth, she admitted that Keith's death was something that she couldn't find a reason for. In chilling honesty, she also stated that she looked forward to the day when she goes to heaven and is with her husband and father again.

With the judgment day seemingly looming a long way

in the future, the CBS television network decided that her life was interesting stuff right at this moment. They assigned a crew and followed Lorrie around for two days for a special edition of *48 Hours*. Dan Rather and his folks were impressed too. The host noted, ''Other styles come and go, country is still around. And sure as corn, it'll be there tomorrow.'' By choosing her, certainly CBS felt that Lorrie would be there tomorrow too. Ratings wise, it probably was no accident that CBS chose a tragic figure who was beautiful to feature, and the folks at home pumped up the network's numbers by tuning in too! So it proved to be a wise choice all the way around.

In May, as ''We Both Walk'' hit the top ten, Lorrie took a brief pause from her own busy life to reach out to a competitor. Morgan stopped her road schedule, re-arranged her personal life, and added another date to raise money for the families of the members of Reba Mc-Entire's band who had recently died in a plane crash. More than anyone else, Lorrie knew the effects of trag-edy. She had felt the pain of not just losing a husband and father, but in seeing a host of Opry stars go down too. Morgan believed that country music was supposed to be a family. So it wasn't surprising that no one seem-ingly wanted to do more to help other musicians in need than she did.

Lorrie's tremendous love for music and her admiration for those who had paved the way for the new stars was probably the reason she figured a way to go back into the studio and work on a Roy Rogers tribute album. The King of the Cowboys, now eighty, was in fine voice as Lorrie joined him on ''Don't Fence Me In.'' And Mor-gan's work helped to make the project a huge success and put a nice finishing touch on one of western music's most illustrious careers. Yet Lorrie wouldn't have con-sidered it a waste of time if the album hadn't sold, she simply thought that singing with a legend was a way to say thanks for what he had given her and everyone else with her music and his class.

Yet Lorrie, the polite young woman who seemed to respect almost all the country music rules and always

honor her elders, was still a bit of rebel too. Not only
did she issue some "damns" and "hells" when she was
being interviewed, but she pretty much ignored many
standards when she felt them working against her own
whim and desires. She would drive a bit over the speed
limit, run over her allotted time on opening shows, and
smoke under No Smoking signs. She would even ignore
the No Smoking sign that hung in the Keith Whitley conference room of the RCA building. And something else
she did often was ignore the advice of friends about the
men in her life.

Still very much on the rebound from the death of her
husband, Lorrie had been opening for Clint Black in the
winter when she met his bus driver Brad Thompson.
Thompson, 31, began dating Lorrie in March. It was she
who asked him out first and even though a host of those
who cared about her urged her to take it slow, Lorrie
kept pushing the relationship. Thompson was divorced
with a nine-year-old daughter of his own, and was hardly
in Morgan's social or maturity class. To many he seemed
more like a puppy following a little kid than he did an
equal part of an adult relationship. Yet in spite of this,
the romance grew. On the road Lorrie waited by the
phone each night just to speak with her honey.

Strangely, because Morgan was now past thirty, in
many ways this new love affair seemed more like a high
school romance than the real thing. Brad and Lorrie were
like two steadies waiting for homecoming. So it was little
wonder that many thought they would last about as long
as high school romances did too. The relationship was
seen as a "make out a little and move on" thing. Yet
Morgan seemed to think of it as something more!

"He is the best thing that ever happened to me," Lorrie declared to *People* magazine in June. "He's gorgeous
and sentimental, very sensitive. He's about 5 foot 9, 160
pounds, long blond hair, pretty blue eyes, and he's just
a blessing." Though many of her friends believed that
she would get bored and leave him soon, at this time
Brad did appear to be bringing Lorrie some easy smiles
and laughs. And that was something that had been miss-

ing from her life for a long time, so the young man was welcomed into the star's inner circle. Still it came as a shock when, less than three months after they first met him, friends found out just how far Brad would be coming into that circle.

Brad had actually asked her to marry him on May 20th in Dallas, Texas. Morgan claimed it was at 8:27 P.M. "I have not felt this way since Keith," she assured her fans at Fan Fair when the duo publicly announced their plans. The couple had chosen October 27, as their wedding date and planned to get hitched in a Nashville Catholic church, St. Joseph's. Even before the words had grown cold, many in Nashville were wagering that the marriage would never happen. And because the date seemed so far in the future, they also weren't too worried about the announcement either. So life went on with the main focus on Morgan's professional side.

In 1991, the TNN/Music City News Awards not only nominated Lorrie, but gave her the award for Vocal Collaboration of the Year. She was also nominated for Single of the Year for " 'Til a Tear Becomes a Rose," as well as Female Artist of the Year. Though she failed to win the latter two awards, she felt she was getting closer to accepting. There was little doubt even in her mind that she was now one of Nashville's most important women. Later in the year, the American Music Awards would also nominate Lorrie for Favorite Female Artist, seemingly proving this view too.

To follow up "We Both Walk," Lorrie and RCA had chosen a country classic. It had been no snap decision either. The label already had decided to issue "A Picture Without You," as the second single even before the first one was released. This number, a remake of an old George Jones hit, would take off quickly on the charts after its August release. Though not as strong on the playlists as "We Both Walk," it would become another top-ten effort for Ms. Morgan. "A Picture" would also bring her a great deal of press and publicity, not all of it kind!

In July, just before the radio stations added the single

to the playlist, Robert K. Oermann noted Lorrie's newest single, "A Picture of Me (Without You)" by writing, "Oh my Gawd, what a record! There are only a handful of singers who could stand to this George Jones classic, look it straight in the eye and sing the fire out of it. Lorrie Morgan does that and creates goosebumps all over your body." If only all the world had seen the release in the way that Oermann had. Yet as right as the song was for Morgan's voice, a host of listeners thought that this release was another attempt by RCA and the singer to trade off of Lorrie's own tragic life.

She told Tulsa writer John Wooley, "Right now, I think no matter what I sing people are going to misinterpret it as being about Keith." In this case, nothing could have been further from the truth. Yet many disc jockeys backed off from really plugging the single because they sensed it was a cheap way to play on people's sympathy. This attitude may have cost Lorrie another number one too. The recording was that good!

In a very real sense Morgan could have used some sympathy. From July to September, Lorrie didn't come home. She lived on the road. The reviewers continued to like her shows, but like the radio disc jockeys, some were growing a bit tired of Morgan's clinging to her ties with Keith Whitley. In particular, many had grown to dislike the taped duets with Whitley. In truth the entire effect now seemed to drag down a solid and uplifting show.

Those in the know suggested that Morgan drop the references to Whitley all together. Even in the face of getting married again, she fought to keep Keith's name out front. Yet even as she was battling to keep Whitley's contribution to her stage show intact, Lorrie was incensed that her own label would cheapen itself in the name of profits by releasing some of Keith's old cuts on a new album.

The new RCA Whitley album was entirely made up of cuts from some of his more unsuccessful sessions. In many of these sessions he had been simply unable to perform up to standards. These were the very efforts that had almost cost him his recording contract in the first

place. When she had first found out about the releases
Lorrie didn't even consider that this was her own label
she was speaking out against, she simply got on her soap
box. It enraged her to have Keith's good work judged
against stuff that he didn't want released when he was
alive. She didn't want his fans to get this second-rate
batch of junk. Yet in spite of her pleas, the label went
ahead with their plans in the name of history. It didn't
prove to be a bad move either. One of the singles,
"Brotherly Love," would slide to number two late in the
year. The other "Somebody's Doin' Me Right," would
also find a solid market in the beginning of 1992. This
issue would ultimately close the door on Keith Whitley's
recording career, but as Lorrie and others would find out,
not his influence.

The Nashville Network approached Lorrie about getting together with them on a first. They wanted to tape
one of the singer's concerts for a special and they wanted
to catch her act on video at the Ryman Auditorium. A
one-person taped concert had never been done before and
TNN figured that to kick off the concept they needed
someone who had a real appreciation for the hallowed
country music venue. Excited, driven, and inspired, Lorrie made magic on that night. Her show and the special
worked and worked well. And to no one's surprise, she
didn't fail to include both of her male influences in the
performance. The crowd that had gathered at the old
Opry house loved "Candy Kisses" too!

In October, Lorrie was again a CMA nominee for Female Vocalist of the Year. Tanya Tucker, who missed
the show because she was having her second baby, won
the honor. And once again the Academy passed on in-
ducting George Morgan into the Hall of Fame. Yet Lorrie
took it all in stride and spent the evening with her beau,
proving to the doubters that she was still making wedding
plans.

As promised, October 27 saw a contract fulfilled at a
church. The critics agreed that Lorrie made a beautiful
bride, but most of the people in attendance didn't see the
spark that Morgan had assured everyone was there. Lor-

rie was going through the motions and saying all the right things, but there didn't seem to be the same kind of passion evident that one saw in her live stage shows. Still this didn't stop *USA Today* and a host of other national publications from covering the event in both pictures and words. Yet it was the words of the singer that may have signaled the way the union was really headed from the start. A hardly blushing Lorrie told a number of different members of the press, "When Brad travels with me, his title is my husband and he takes care of me." In more blunt words, that was his job. Once again the images of a puppy following a child came to mind.

She would later admit that in spite of the beautiful ceremony, things didn't start well. Almost immediately Morgan began having female problems. She said that during that time she was not easy to live with. And though the couple had managed to make some time for themselves, Lorrie had spent a great deal of the early part of their marriage in the hospital. Eventually her medical problems would result in a hysterectomy (and this would be blamed for ending another well-publicized romance). Brad's timing just couldn't have been much worse, and because of Lorrie's health, the weaknesses in their relationship were revealed much more quickly that they probably otherwise would have been. Yet coming on the heels of her second husband's death, and still caught up in a career that needed good publicity, Morgan couldn't afford for this union to fail as quickly as it has begun. And like everything else in her life, she worked hard to find the magic to keep it going. Yet as "Except for Monday" began to climb the charts around Christmas, Lorrie found her private life was anything but merry. The world didn't know that yet, and the world would not know that for quite some time either.

Chapter 12

Lorrie Morgan had scored a top-ten record with "Except for Monday." The single was the third from her second LP. That album, *Something in Red,* had been on playlists for almost a year and had already moved past gold and was heading toward platinum status. So undoubtedly, based on reviews and solid sales, there was a tremendous amount of enthusiasm at RCA when the "Something in Red" single was finally released. The label and critics had long believed this cut to be one of the greatest country songs ever written. Coupled with a video that was clearly one of the most beautiful and dramatic ever shot (Who ever looked better in a sexy red dress than Lorrie?), and with a host of fans already calling radio stations asking for this spin from the album, "Red" seemed like a sure fire number one. As it turned out, the video was. It ruled at CMT. Yet the single didn't seem to play well on radio. Though the most-requested song during her concerts, "Something in Red" didn't mark up the numbers that many expected, barely crawling into the top twenty.

No one seemed to have the answer as to why "Red" didn't become the "Song of the Year." It seemed as if everything was in place to make it happen. Lorrie was hot, the video was torrid, and the album was selling at light speed. So why didn't radio buy into it? Ultimately what might have killed it was that it was a woman's song. And even though a majority of those who bought country music were women, a majority of those who programmed the playlists were men. A lot of them preferred "Rednecks, White Socks, and Blue Ribbon Beer" over a pretty new outfit.

As winter gave way to spring, many were wondering

if Morgan wasn't beginning to cool off. They figured if she couldn't make a hit with production and promotion like ''Something in Red'' had gotten, then it must have signaled the beginning of the downhill slide. Yet the public did perceive it that way. As usual they disagreed with some of the experts, and also as usual, those who bought the product were proven correct.

At the very moment when ''Red'' was not making the expected waves, Lorrie hosted the nationally televised Academy of Country Music awards show. Her cohosts were Clint Black and Travis Tritt. Early in the show Lorrie was nominated for the Female Vocalist award, and as usual she didn't win. Yet Morgan ran the show so smoothly that most forget that she didn't take home a trophy. Unlike the two men with whom she worked, she looked cool and collected and showed not even a hint of nerves. It appeared as if she was having a ball, and she claimed that she was. In the end, she probably won more by hosting than the award winners did by winning. The exposure was terrific. And Hollywood, the program's home, had noticed the sexy and talented blonde too! With L.A. calling, would Morgan soon join Dolly Parton and take a stroll with the studio, leaving Music City behind?

If she decided to go Hollywood or not, in a real sense, with her national recognition, superstar status and millions in record sales, Lorrie had finally out-grown the Opry. There had been a time when Dolly had said goodbye, and now it seemed it was time for Lorrie to do the same. After all just regularly working the show was costing her hundreds of thousands of dollars each year. Yet unlike so many others who went charging out to take advantage of the opportunity for the big bucks, Lorrie stayed home. In her mind, no show was more important that the Saturday night show at the Opry.

''It's funny,'' she said when it was pointed out that she did not have to have the Opry anymore. ''The longer I do this, the stronger I feel about the Grand Ole Opry. There's just this tremendous sense of roots and family there—and being connected to that is so grounding. It really keeps you focused on what's important because if you cut off the roots, the tree dies, no matter how healthy it is.'' Lorrie wasn't ready to die yet either and she wasn't going to sell out the tree either.

Morgan had a new marriage that was making news by summer (not the one to the now all but invisible Brad Thompson). In a shock to many, RCA and Lorrie had parted company after two hugely successful albums, and Lorrie had signed with BNA. For all those who were used to purchasing her product, this looked like a serious move. It would have been like Mickey Mantle leaving the Yankees for the expansion Mets in 1962. Yet in reality it wasn't as much a move as the uninformed public believed. BNA was simply a new country division of RCA. Still Lorrie's new contract was played for all it was worth (and that was millions).

''Although I regret not being able to work in a creative capacity with Lorrie,'' stated RCA president Thom Schuyler in a press release. ''Logic dictates that her producer, Richard Landis, and the BNA label should be responsible parties. Lorrie is a great artist and a magnificent vocalist who has always recorded wonderfully written songs. The staff at RCA has created the kind of atmosphere necessary to help pave Lorrie's way to become a platinum artist in this very competitive time in country music. It's where she deserves to be. We are all behind her 100 percent.''

Thom didn't sound too much like the forsaken lover.

Lorrie added, ''I'm very excited about my move to BNA. I'm deeply grateful to RCA for helping me build what I consider a great foundation for my career. I'll still be a part of BMG and this has made my decision much easier. I'm looking forward to my new family at BNA Entertainment and a great future together.''

Lorrie didn't sound too much like a woman leaving a bad marriage either.

Ric Pepin, BNA's general manager then concluded the press gathering. ''Lorrie Morgan is a superstar and BNA stands prepared to devote a great deal of focus on her career. We feel it is in the best interest of Lorrie Morgan as an artist and in the best interest of BMG as a company to have Lorrie Morgan on our small yet fast-growing label.''

Ric didn't sound like the guy who had just stolen Cinderella from Prince Charming either.

Never had a divorce and second marriage ceremony gone so smoothly. It was as if the ex-spouse was giving the bride away to the new mate. Then they both headed toward the same honeymoon suite all arm-in-arm. Only in the music business could a move like this happen. To the common person on the street, this whole thing must have seemed stupid, even if RCA and BNA were both under the corporate umbrella of BMG. RCA was like General Motors, and BNA was like Saturn. Would this move really enhance Morgan's career, which had stalled a bit when ''Something in Red'' had only climbed to number fourteen? Only time and product would tell.

Lorrie's first single for BNA, ''Watch Me,'' proved that Morgan's career was still worth watching and her move across the corporate hall had not been ill-conceived. Once again using her proven formula of hot videos accompanying each release, the beautiful Morgan climbed back into the top five. Her final number two standing was her highest since ''Five Minutes'' went number one two years before.

A lot of the first BNA album had Lorrie's old RCA ''Red'' feel. This was no accident. BNA knew it didn't need to fix something that wasn't broken. Morgan described her initial release as ''a very fun song. It's fun to do on stage, it was a fun video to make, and it was my first experience with a real actor, Rick Rossovich, who was my husband in this video. The video actually ends on a very upbeat note. It's got a happy ending, and that's what I like to think of when I'm performing the song anyway, that it does have a happy ending.'' Yet Lorrie and BNA didn't even think that ''Watch Me'' was anywhere near the best thing they had to offer from the project.

When pressed about the *Watch Me* LP, there were a lot of other cuts that Lorrie wanted to preview as well, both in concert with music and in interviews via description.

The fact was that Lorrie was excited, and why not, her last two efforts had proven that had that Midas touch and this *Watch Me* album was simply a return to those days. She might have not pulled down the big awards, and "Red" might have stalled a bit, but the singer still knew that she had a growing fan base that would remain loyal. This fan base had always wanted her product, and now they would have more than one choice too!

Even as the new album hit the market, Lorrie was talking about another one too. After only two albums, Lorrie Morgan and her label were already putting out a *Greatest Hits* LP. With two releases and the singles they spanned flooding the market, there was so much about which to talk. Lorrie hardly knew where to start. Yet as always, when speaking of her own recordings, the first thing she had to mention was emotion.

"Artists need to be moved to tears by their own songs," she explained as she reviewed her *Greatest Hits* concept. "Over the years, it's seemed that my favorite songs, the ones that really get me, are always the fans' favorites too."

Anyone who had appeared in the top ten eight times in three years seemed to have a handle on what folks liked. And maybe a great deal of that was because she was so picky when reviewing material. When she had first gotten a chance at RCA, her producer had advised her to sing songs she could really get into. Four albums later she had made a success out of doing just that. The *Watch Me* album proved that she was traveling this road again, and Greatest Hits was a statement to prove that the path she had traveled had embraced this concept in the past as well.

"I get to make about an album a year," she pointed out in press interviews. "That's ten songs, which really isn't very many. If I'm going to make a record, I want to make sure they're songs that really speak to me. They have to; because even if it's something playful, it's a spot I could be using for something else. And I think that's the difference between cutting great songs that matter to you and songs that are hits just because they're hits.''

She continued this line of thought by reviewing her new efforts and tying them to her life's journey. Her comments not only showed just how closely she kept tabs on her music, but her own life too.

''I think 'I Didn't Know My Own Strength' really does sum it up. That's where I am in my own life right now. I'm releasing my *Greatest Hits*—and I never thought I'd be doing that so soon in my career. But then, all I've ever done was focus on what needed to be done and keep going. When that's how you work, it's easy to miss the ground you're covering.''

Again and again, Morgan came back to the one-step-at-a-time concept that had kept her from collapsing and giving up when Keith had died. It was this one-step-at-a-time concept that had allowed her to endure the mourning as well as the court battles. It was that one-step-at-a-time concept that had seen her putting together a second great album and putting on a happy face even when she felt like dying. And it was that one-step-at-a-time approach that kept her focused on her children and her role as a mother even before her highly charged and successful career.

When Morgan had been at the top, she had seen the bottom. And during that time, Lorrie had learned that she couldn't answer all of her problems at once, nor could she answer all of the questions at once either, but she could take them one at a time and do pretty well. And just like she had refused to give up the Opry and other things in which she believed, she could accomplish great things without compromise either.

''That's one of the things I really liked about 'Standing Tall,' '' Morgan explained. ''It's a song about refusing to give up my self-respect. (When you're in a relationship) it's so easy to cave in and go against your own judgment, but it's just as easy to be strong and stand tall. You always have to keep that in mind.''

Maybe it was because she had been forced to lift her five-foot-two-inch frame up so high so many times that this tune was to become her theme song. After all, there seemed to be a hundred different moments, even back to when she tried to start her career and get involved with the Opry, that she was the only one standing up for herself. Yet as the years went by the more she realized that she wasn't alone either. There were a lot of people facing difficult times who had to stand up tall in order to make it through one more day.

"For a lot of women, that's just how it is," Lorrie pointed out. "But that's the thing about women today too. Because of this, they're strong and have this fullness of who they are. They're single moms. They're working. They're living their lives. And they have all these things to bring to a relationship, if they so choose. Given that, it's an exciting time to be singing songs to and about women."

With that in mind, "What Part of No," her second release for BNA, was a classic country song and a perfect way for Lorrie to end the year and give a message to all of her women fans. This single said what every woman needed to say at least once every day in order to survive in a man's world, and it said it so well, that when "What Part of No" peaked, it would knock one of country music's hottest young studs, Travis Tritt, out of the top spot. This single would stay number one for three weeks and lead a charge for Morgan's *Watch Me* album to earn a Gold status. So Lorrie had good reason to be constantly bragging on her new label in concerts and interviews. She soon found out that the feeling was mutual too.

Ric Pepin of BNA couldn't say enough about Lorrie. She was his star. And why shouldn't he feel that way. Lorrie was jumpstarting this new arm of the RCA label in a manner that few companies had ever seen. She was making the label very well-known in a hurry. A lot of BNA's quick success could be traced directly to Lorrie Morgan. And though the awards were not coming as quickly as they would have liked, the label didn't pay its employees with awards. It paid them with hits. And Morgan's great sales paid a lot of the hired help.

Still, the hits notwithstanding, at the CMA awards

show, BNA's superstar was passed over again, this time for folk/country singer Mary Chapin Carpenter. Carpenter, a talented singer/song writer held a far different image than Morgan did. Mary Chapin was tomboyish, dressed that way, and appealed to the college crowd. As the sexy Lorrie stood beside the somewhat dowdy Carpenter, there was no doubt as to who turned heads. Yet the votes were cast for the woman singing the ''newest'' kind of country music, not the one whom *Playboy* wanted between their pages.

Partly because of being passed over for awards, partly because of her crumbling marriage and continuing health problems, partly from simply pushing too hard, by October Morgan was completely bushed. Perform, record, do interviews, travel, grab something to eat, smoke an endless chain of cigarettes, and in the time that was left, be a mother. Deep down she had to question just how her father had done it back when things were even harder. Where had he found the time to rest? Was this why his heart gave out so young?

Even though she had sworn that she would never pay the high price of deeding her life over to the star system, in fact Lorrie was spending too much time working. She was wearing down. She would often tell her band, ''I'm just too damn tired.'' And even though her shows were still top shelf, she often was so worn down that when she wasn't in front of audience, she was too beat to do anything she really enjoyed.

It was obvious to survive with any kind of good mental or physical health, Lorrie was going to have to get some time to herself. She was going to have to cut back. Yet those all around her were pushing her forward. They wanted her to do even more. As she looked ahead to 1993, Lorrie had to ask all those who were giving her constant marching orders the same question that was the title of her latest hit, ''What Part of No'' do you not understand?

Chapter 13

After several roller coaster years of extreme highs and lows, 1993 would have neither. Though the year had initially offered great promises in matters concerning both her career and her professional life, Lorrie would spend a great deal of those twelve months just working to hold her ground. As she was so near the top of her profession, staying even was not that bad, but it wasn't especially good either. To many, because Morgan was no longer country music's hottest new female star, her inability to make another upwardly mobile move signaled that the performer might have just peaked. And peaking was just about the most frightening accomplishment that any musician could imagine.

The year that Lorrie held her own was the year that TNN decided to get involved in the business of making movies. The highly successful television programmer sensed that those who watched the network, as well as those who followed country music in general, would tune in to view telemovies, which featured country music's hottest new stars. When reviewing scripts and concepts, as well as negotiating with managers, one name kept popping up in conversations as the country music star to kick off this concept. It seemed that almost everyone in town thought that this one performer was a "can't miss" star. So, when the final decision came down, it was hardly surprising that TNN embraced Lorrie Morgan to grace their first feature. After all, Music City's movers and shakers, even those who didn't especially care for Lorrie, agreed that this seemed to be a good idea.

There would seem to be little doubt that Morgan's easy style on videos helped them come to that decision. In

mini-movies such as "Something in Red" and "Dear
Me," Lorrie had projected the ability to emote like an
"real" actress. The viewers always seemed to buy into
her performance.

Lorrie was also a "zapper stopper"—someone who
kept channel surfers from going on to the next channel.
This was a quality that really excited TNN. And because
she acted with such seeming ease in her videos, it just
didn't seem that Morgan was going to need a lot of
coaching either. So when she was viewed as a commodity, Lorrie was deemed as good-looking, had a great
speaking voice, and had a strong following among the
huge fan base that made up the TNN demographic group.
In other words, it seemed that she was the "total package." With any kind of script, Morgan would seem to
assure the producers good ratings.

It hadn't been hard to sell the singer on the idea of
starring in TNN's first feature either. Lorrie had long ex-
pressed an interest in acting. What had probably held her
back was not wanting to have to work for months at a
time in Los Angeles. Lorrie was a Nashville girl, and
whenever she stayed away from home for very long, she
missed the city. Yet when an opportunity to stay home
and work as an actress was presented to her, she jumped
at the chance.

Lorrie would explain that taking the acting role was
good for her as it would place her in a position to grow.
Meeting new challenges in new areas of discovery was
like going back to school for Morgan. And because this
opportunity would put her in an unfamiliar setting, she
would have to learn and produce at the same time. While
Lorrie loved to function under this kind of pressure, it
was doubtful that she realized just how unfamiliar and
uncomfortable this new setting was really going to be.
Still, even if she had fully realized what was in store for
her, she probably wouldn't have reconsidered.

Onstage Lorrie was always comfortable. Onstage she
called all the shots. Yet when she took her stab at acting,
she quickly found that she was always at the mercy of
others. She was no longer her own boss. She had abso-

lutely no control over anything, from the script to her schedule. Letting go of the control over even a small bit of her life had always been very hard on Morgan, so the movie was a killer. Yet like everything else she committed to, she worked through it and gave the somewhat weak script and cheap production her all. In the end she hoped that she hadn't embarrassed herself.

Proudheart aired in August and Lorrie found that she was satisfied with her performance. Yet the telemovie was not what TNN had envisioned it was going to be. The facts were that *Proudheart* was neither a critical nor commercial success. While it was true that this story of a poor but strong woman fighting against tough breaks and tough times was nominated for a Cable Ace award, most cable viewers still somehow missed hearing about it. Worst of all, they missed it in spite of a great publicity campaign. It seemed that when the producer and director wiped away Lorrie's glamour to fit the script's humble lead, they also killed much of the singer's ability to stop the channel surfers. That was like killing the golden goose or discarding the trump card in a card game. Yet even while *Proudheart* signaled the beginning and end of TNN's efforts at producing its own theatrical features, it seemed to be a good break for Morgan. She had gotten a chance to discover that she was no Meryl Streep. But for the first time out of the box she wasn't that bad either, and because of that chance at a new area of performing, she had appreciated the experience. Still, she ended the picture wondering if she would ever want to release that much control over her affairs again.

In April, Lorrie quietly announced that she was divorcing Brad Thompson. It seemed that no matter how hard the couple worked at their marriage, Lorrie found that the bus driver simply couldn't live up to Keith's image. The breakup was no surprise to her fans or friends, and most were relieved to see it happen. They sensed that Morgan could do far better.

Lorrie explained that the union simply was not strong enough to survive the pressures of her career. She cited, "A mutual parting of the ways," as the official reason for the divorce. Yet the real reason was probably more akin to the singer understanding that Brad had been little more than a rebound romance. He was good-looking, but looks didn't matter over the phone or in the dark. She needed more. And so even though accepting a part of the blame was a risky career move, as the two went their separate ways, Lorrie was ready to admit that she had made another mistake. It was almost that simple. And so was the divorce. Morgan sealed her split with Brad Thompson by purchasing him a new pick-up and giving him $65,000. All things considered, it was a pretty cheap settlement. Ultimately, because Brad had been so low profile, the press didn't make much of it either.

A few weeks after the divorce, Lorrie was decked out—low-cut and fit to kill—at the Academy of Country Music Awards show. Troy Aikman, the quarterback of the World Champion Dallas Cowboys, was on her arm and flashbulbs were popping everywhere the couple turned. From sports shows to *Entertainment Tonight,* everyone in the media wanted to know where and how the two had gotten together.

It may have been to avoid the tabloid press gossip or to assure those who cared about her that she wasn't on the rebound again, but at first Morgan simply called Aikman a very good friend. She had met the grid-iron star through Marty Raybon of Shenandoah at a recent golf benefit. Marty and Troy had been close for years, and the Dallas Cowboy had even appeared in several of the group's videos. Yet soon Lorrie and Troy would have something that Marty couldn't claim.

To those around them, it seemed that Troy was hooked on Lorrie from the first moment they met. The two seemed to have a great many common interests. They also both had very public lives, but were basically shy people who had come to treasure their times away from the spotlight. And both of them appeared to be on the professional upswing. The only matters which seemed to work against the extremely attractive duo was the fact that the singer was several years older than the jock, and that Lorrie had been through three marriages, while Troy had never walked down the aisle even once. Yet those problems aside, from the moment the public first got a glimpse of them, the duo was hot!

In a very real sense, the couple stole the thunder of every major act who appeared on the show. It was Lorrie and Troy who were the night's big news, not who won what award. That evening Lorrie would cohost the ACMs for the second year in a row, but to fully understand how unimportant an honor that was—as compared to being on Aikman's arm—you would have heard Morgan sing her new release, "I Guess You Had to Be There." Win or lose, the singer was there, and she looked as if she was enjoying every minute of it too! Millions of women would have loved to have traded places with her.

At the 1993 ACMs, Lorrie might have lost the female vocalist award to Mary Chapin Carpenter, but because of Aikman, no one seemed to notice. And Morgan didn't even really seem to care either. It looked as if she realized, that while she might have struck out in the awards chase, that was minor-league stuff. By simply being on Troy's arm, Morgan had won the show.

A month later the papers and tabloids were abuzz with the news of the new coupling between the quarterback and the singer. Not all the news reports were glowing tributes to the power of love. Some were saying that the singer was on a secret mission to distract Aikman and keep him from playing up to standards in the next football campaign. Other sports scribes wondered how hard the quarterback would be training in the off season when he seemed to be going everywhere with Lorrie. For some reason, especially in Dallas, Morgan was almost viewed as a black widow. Yet the spidery image didn't scare Troy. He couldn't get enough of the sexy siren.

Besides the daily onslaught of press about her dating life, most of it unwanted, Lorrie was now also getting a host of new questions about her music. For the first time in almost three years critics and fans were not seeing a "Keith's dead" element in every one of her releases. Many reporters were even asking Morgan if she was singing for today's woman. With songs like "What Part

of No'' and ''Something in Red,'' the fans and critics
had a reason to see Lorrie as a role model for the breed
of women who had so much to do and so little time to
do it. For the singer, this ''today's woman image'' was
one of the few lines of questioning that had to seem re-
freshing. In a sense, Morgan was relieved that after the
last few years having everyone wonder if every song she
did was in reaction to the death of her late husband, that
now she could move on to other reasons to sing and other
statements to make.

The fact was that Lorrie liked being suddenly considered the spokesperson for the average American female.
But to her credit, Morgan didn't spend a great deal of
time dwelling on how tough her life really was. She said
that while what she did was far different than most
women, the fact that she had to leave her children to go
to work, and that work caused her to miss some of life's
most important moments, was not that different than what
millions of women working out in the real world went
through each day. Maybe this was true, but few of the
millions of women who looked to Morgan as a symbol
of strength got to go home with an NFL quarterback.

With Aikman almost constantly at her side, with her
records still making noise on the charts, with her role as
an actress in the can, and knowing that she had rid her
life of the mistake that had been her third husband, Morgan was on a roll. She was thrilling huge crowds with
her music and her stage presence, appearing each night
in a magical puff of smoke, wearing sexy outfits and
dispensing a great deal of humor with her songs. She was
even being recognized by groups such as the National
Cosmetology Association as the nation's top stylemaker,
beating out the likes of Demi Moore, Reba McEntire, and
Hillary Rodham Clinton for the honor. After having so
many years when tragedy and unhappiness hung over her
life like a dark cloud, now it was almost like everyday
was Christmas. To prove that point, Lorrie even tried to
make it seem that way too!

Lorrie Morgan loved Christmas like few people did.

This was the one time of the year when everyone, including her father, had been home at the same time. To Lorrie, it had always meant family, church, presents, and singing. As a matter of fact, ''Silent Night'' was George Morgan's favorite song and he had sung it at every Christmas Opry show.

Therefore it was not unusual that Lorrie had long dreamed of cutting a Christmas album, but those who knew Lorrie also knew that she wasn't interested in doing it the same way almost everyone else in Music City did. As always it seemed that Lorrie had her own ideas. And they were big ones too! She wanted to go to England and record in London with the New World Philharmonic Orchestra. She also wanted to invite some folks like Andy Williams, Johnny Mathis, and Tammy Wynette to join her. It was a tall order that probably would have been ignored except for the fact that Lorrie was BNA's superstar artist and the label felt as if they owed it to her. Besides, even if the album didn't light up the stores in the manner that Lorrie's other products had, the BNA felt sure that her fans would buy enough to turn a profit.

''The main reason I wanted to do a Christmas album is because the holiday is such a very special part of my life,'' Lorrie had explained to the media through the BNA publicity machine. ''Growing up with Mom and Dad and three older sisters and an older brother, Christmas was a total fantasy time for me when I was a child. I've tried to keep that fantasy alive for my children so that their memories are as grand and as cherished as mine. Some day, when I'm long gone, hopefully the memories and this Christmas album will continue as a part of their lives.''

Richard Landis again was chosen to produce the work. To make Lorrie's big dream into a reality, he brought in eighty-two musicians and singers. He also assigned Charlie Calello, an arranger who had worked with the likes of Barbra Streisand, Frank Sinatra, Engelbert Humperdinck, Lou Christie, Glen Campbell, and the Four Seasons, to put together the new arrangements. Landis knew just how much this album meant to Lorrie, so he tried not to leave a single stone unturned.

"First of all," Richard noted, "Lorrie Morgan has probably more affection for and knowledge of Christmas music than anyone I've ever met. I mean she knows them all. She had at least twenty ideas, so we had to edit down from that and figure out which ones would fit this style. After all, she wanted something on a grand scale."

When he heard that she was interested in having him join her on the project, Andy Williams called Lorrie at home. She played him "Little Snow Girl" over the phone.

"He had never heard it," Lorrie remembered. "So I said, 'the only copy I've got is on an album, and the stereo is in my daughter's room isn't the greatest, but I'll try to play it for you.' So I held up the receiver to the speaker and played Andy Williams the song I wanted to record with him. He loved it and agreed."

Johnny Mathis had long loved Lorrie's voice and the superstar had a deep understanding of her relationship with her father, as he too had learned to sing from his dad. When Lorrie wrote Johnny asking him if he would take a few days to help her out, he announced that he would love to work with her, but only if he got to record something he had never cut before. Lorrie suggested "Blue Snowfall," a song which George Morgan had once recorded. Morgan sent the song to Mathis, and the singer fell in love with it.

"Singing with Lorrie Morgan was a two-fold pleasure," Johnny explained. "First because of God-given talent and her kindness to me. Second because of her love for her father and his singing."

Another special moment came when Lorrie cut "Up on Santa Claus Mountain," a song which her father had written.

"We only had one copy of the song," Lorrie recalled, "and it was a cassette that dad had done years and years ago at my uncle's house. It wasn't even done at the studio." Landis and Lorrie worked out a new arrangement for the old song and scored it in a way that George would

have probably never even imagined in his wildest
dreams.

With an almost nine-minute medley closing out the LP,
it was a high-dollar, serious attempt to bring Christmas
spirit home to the listener. Lorrie wanted it to be just as
perfect as the Christmases she had when George had
pulled out the guitar and the family had sung the songs
of the season. When she listened to the final product, she
knew that she had accomplished just that. Her big dreams
had been realized. This was an album that had caught
and preserved the true spirit of the season.

Even as she was working on her Christmas project, "I
Guess You Had to Be There" managed to move into the
top twenty, hitting only number fourteen. The final numbers for the song weren't that bad, but they were down
a notch or two from her old numbers. If this became a
trend, then it might signal problems too. So this failure
to make the top ten would have seemed to be a sign for
at least a bit of worry, and behind the scenes, BNA was
looking at the new album's potential problems.

In a sense, *War Paint*, the title for Lorrie's second
BNA regular LP, didn't seem to connect with her fans
and the critics the way that her first three projects (as
well as *Greatest Hits*) had. No one was expecting this
letdown either. There had been high hopes for *Paint* going in. A great deal of this positive anticipation was based
on how much Morgan had thrown herself into this work.
Because she had been heavily involved in every facet of
War Paint and because she seemed to know her fans so
well, BNA had a reason to feel confident. Lorrie felt
good, so they did too!

"I try to grow with every album," she had explained
when the product was shipped. "I try to find songs that
say something about what I feel, songs that deal with the
things people feel in their lives. And this time, I was able
to say it with songs that are mine. I can't think of a better
way to grow."

In an effort to make this new work a strong and personal statement, Lorrie had even been pushed back into
writing some of the cuts on it. This attempt to put her

own emotions and thoughts into the package came about largely because of the influence of Kris Kristofferson. Her publicist, Susan Nader, had informed Kristofferson that Lorrie was a pretty solid writer who simply didn't have enough faith in her own stuff. Nader talked Kris into demanding that Lorrie share some of her songs with him. When Kris and Lorrie had worked on a video together off of her third album, he did just that.

"It took me forever to be able to play in front of him," Lorrie admitted, "and then when I did, I was just shaking inside. And he sat there listening with his head down, really concentrating, although all I could think was that he didn't like it.

"When I finished, he looked up and said, 'Lorrie, a lot of people are writers. Few are poets. You're a poet.' I still can't get over Kris saying that." Yet ultimately, the personally penned song of which she was most proud would be one that the public and the disc jockeys believed that the world simply didn't need.

Outside of writing her own stuff, one of Lorrie's favorite moments from the project came when she worked with Allison Krauss and Pam Tillis on "The Hard Part Was Easy." Little did Morgan know that in just two years, she and Pam would be reunited in a nationwide tour with another performer whose country music roots had been an important part of country music history. At this point the song was simply thought of as a once-in-a-lifetime opportunity for Mel's daughter and George's daughter to be caught on tape together.

Even with the merging of a great deal of talent and money, even with Lorrie dressed as a sexy Indian maiden on the jacket, *War Paint* still wasn't strong enough to come close to her first efforts. With each release, this became more evident. "Half Enough," the next single, did strike into the lower half of the top ten, peaking at number eight. Yet just like the LP's other releases, it was destined to become a song that fans didn't love like they had "Dear Me" or "Five Minutes."

"My Night to Howl," the single after "Half Enough," was a successful and very sexy video. It seemed that

Lorrie in a cat suit was something that viewers couldn't get enough of on TNN and CMT. Even Batman would have loved it! Yet radio stations didn't sell this kind of visual imagery. It only managed to salvage a brief stint in the bottom of the top forty.

In an act that many viewed as desperation or just plain poor taste, BNA next shipped a song that Lorrie had written about Keith Whitley. Fans and radio programmers seemed to really feel uncomfortable listening to this cut.

"If You Come Back from Heaven," a self-penned tribute to Lorrie's continuing love for Keith Whitley, was a sad and morbidly strange reminder of how much Morgan loved and missed her husband. Yet from the stale response, it seemed obvious that not everyone longed for Keith to return. To most fans, his music was now a part of the past of country music. And even the inspiration of having Lorrie wonder what it would be like if he could have returned, didn't strike up a common note with the fans. This kind of thinking was a leap of faith that they were no longer willing to make. It didn't mean that they didn't care, it only meant that they had moved on. They wanted to know what was going on with Troy. Not even the press was interested in talking about Whitley now. So Keith Whitley's memory was not going to help the new LP sell either.

War Paint would go gold, but those sales numbers were a big step down from Lorrie's previous three conceptional album efforts. Was this the beginning of the end? In a world where country acts faded even more quickly than they appeared, was Morgan heading down the mountain like Randy Travis and Ricky Van Shelton recently had? Could she rally her forces and turn around the quickening slide? More importantly, did she really want too?

"I don't want to be old at thirty-five," Lorrie told *Music City News*. Yet the pace she was living seemed to be heading her in that direction. In 1993 she had 115 concerts, scores of television shows, a long continuing round of benefits for alcohol and drug programs, fan meetings, a divorce, a movie, well-publicized dates with

America's favorite team's most eligible bachelor, softball games, a growing role as a mom, and an ongoing fight to keep the news on her life straight. With that list, it would seem that her time to sleep would have been numbered in moments, not hours. With the need to cut back written on her tired face, with female problems still plaguing her, maybe a slide in popularity might be just what the doctor ordered. Yet as would soon be proven, this was not what the singer had in mind. She didn't want to hold her own or slide out of the spotlight, she wanted to be even hotter than she had been in 1991 and 1992. In sense, she wanted her cake and her cowboy too. The question was, ''Could she manage it?''

Chapter 14

In 1994 Lorrie talked with journalist Kimmy Wix as she looked back at the first three and half decades of her life. In an excellently written piece in the bible of country music, *The Music City News*, Wix related what Morgan had shared with the writer about survival amidst tragedy.

"I think my main strength is my sense of humor," Lorrie explained to Kimmy. "I think I was raised that way—that without a sense of humor, you take yourself and life too seriously." It may have just been that sense of humor that had pulled Lorrie through times that had caused lesser men and women to give it up and pack it in. Yet the question the singer now had to answer was not "Can I make it through any more tough times?" but rather, "Have I peaked?"

One of the ways to measure that she probably hadn't become a part of yesterday's boring news was the growing interest the tabloid press continued to have in her private life. True or not, the lurid Lorrie stories kept flooding in week after week. The pace had even picked up since the appearance at the Academy of Country Music show with Troy Aikman. So, much more than anyone else in country music, even those like Shania Twain who were ever so hot on the charts, Lorrie sold magazines at the check-out lines. These stories may have kept Morgan's name in the public eye and showed that she was still a fan favorite, but the fact that a great many of the tales in those scandal sheets centered on the singer's love affair with Aikman was now creating problems in her private life.

The Dallas Cowboy quarterback was a vibrant facet of every bit of Lorrie's life. It seemed that Troy was everything that Brad was not. He was her knight in shining armor. Tall, good-looking, and in no way tied to the music business, he was everything she had ever dreamed of in her Prince Charming. And he was always there for her. Yet just being there was causing a problem for the younger man. Troy was simply not used to the constant spotlight like Lorrie was. Football was much different than show business. His life with Lorrie was not just a sixteen-week-a-year gig in front of millions for just one day of those sixteen weeks. It was everyday. There was no time off. He had to be "on" all the time. And as the months went by and the tabloids kept digging deeper for more and more stories, it became increasingly hard for Morgan to hold onto her quarterback. When no one could block the blitzing media, he wanted to run away and hide.

It seemed that Aikman didn't just hate the stories about him and Lorrie, he despised them. It sickened him to see his private life spread all over the supermarket check-out lanes. He didn't like the kidding he was getting from friends, teammates, and sports reporters either. And the fact that the couple spent so much time away from each other was something else that caused him to believe that Lorrie was just not worth the effort.

To her credit, the singer was willing to leave Nashville and move to Dallas if that is what Troy felt their relationship needed. For Morgan to even consider such a move was incredible. Music City was her home. Leaving would not just put a strain on her career, but separate her from her siblings and mother. And what about the Opry? How could she continue to work on a regular basis there if she lived in Texas? Yet she was willing to give all of that up for Troy. All he had to do was ask. Ultimately the shy grid-iron star never would.

Lorrie's continuing medical problems finally forced her into the hospital again in 1994. Beside her was Aikman. The mere fact that he was there watching the singer endure the agony of a hysterectomy signaled more than the end of Morgan's child-bearing possibilities. It also signaled the beginning of the end of her relationship with

Troy. Troy wanted children and Lorrie couldn't fulfill that wish anymore. Without that promise, the football player and singer would find that their fairy-tale romance had become nothing more than a story with an unhappy ending. As the cowboy rode off into the sunset, Lorrie felt pain and heartache like none she had felt since Keith had died.

Lorrie would tell *USA Today*'s Dick Zimmerman that she had been hurt so much because she was so often willing to give it her all. Yet even while the pain of loss had seemingly enveloped so much of her life, it also had helped to establish her too. Though not spoken of, in a sense, the heartaches had given her a chance to be something other than a second-generation country music wannabe. Her father's death had first put her in the spotlight. Her husband's death had again put the spotlight on her. And now her relationship with Troy had accomplished the same thing. It was a strange kind of curse, one that constantly broke her heart while giving her more and more chances at fame. And she was famous everywhere. After all, when *USA Today* did a cover story on you, you had made it to a pretty recognizable level.

In the *USA Today* article, Zimmerman called Lorrie "country's sexiest beauty." There is no doubt that her Marilyn Monroe-type appearance had helped her in an age where being wholesome had been replaced by being hot. To capitalize on her beauty, the singer had come out with a best-selling swimsuit calender. Even the stars of *Baywatch* had to be looking over their shoulders at the former girlfriend of a football star. Envy was not what drove Lorrie to come out with a pin up calendar. What pushed her was business. She knew that sex sold, but she was also wise enough to know where to draw the line and to realize that it took talent to continue to sell year after year.

While giving a big nod to her looks, Zimmerman pointed out that Lorrie's life and music always touched a wide range of emotions too. When she sang in one of her low-cut gowns, she caused both "hormones and heartaches" to rage. Lorrie might have modestly laughed

off the quote in public, but in truth she had worked hard
to cultivate this image. This was the combination of sex
and talent that she had hoped to capture as her own. This
was the corner of the country music market she wanted
for herself.

"I don't consider myself a sexpot or anything like
that," Lorrie told Zimmerman, "but I don't think there's
anything wrong in dressing and looking like a woman."
One look at her calendar seemed to assure most everyone
that she *did* believe in looking like a woman, and a very
beautiful one at that. And maybe in part because of that
fact, even with Aikman running a fade route, the press
was still interested in Lorrie Morgan.

In March, a now healthy Lorrie joined forces with her
old mentor George Jones in hosting the Music City News
Country Songwriter Awards. Many wondered how Morgan would endure working with Jones again. Her first
stint with him had been like taking a tour through Hell.
But during the press conference, Lorrie had nothing but
nice things to say about the old master. She seemed to
have forgotten all the horror stories that had punctuated
her eighteen months on the road with Jones. Now she
only recalled the good times.

These songwriter awards, broadcast on TNN, meant a
lot to Lorrie. If they hadn't, she wouldn't have taken the
time out to host them. She was currently getting enough
exposure in the press and on television that appearing on
the program was not something her career really needed.
Rather, in this case, she was again giving up some of her
free days to honor a part of her country music family.
Lorrie knew the real power of well-written songs. She
had been raised to appreciate the talents of these story-
tellers. Morgan felt it was important to honor those
whose music touched hearts. And those who watched the
show that night, many of them had tuned in to see the
singer or what she would be wearing, quickly realized
that this woman really did appreciate every winner that
night. Yet in a world filled with more and more demands,
with more and more people pulling on her, this was one

of the few times when she seemed to really get to do something that she wanted to do.

At first becoming a star had simply meant a loss of time and privacy. Then Lorrie had been discovered by the tabloid press and being a star meant living with lies and half-truths that millions believed as the gospel. Then being a superstar meant long hours, hard work, and not much time to enjoy her hard-earned money. And now it was getting worse! No matter how much things had changed, no matter that the press corps had gone from a few to hundreds, no matter that now there was often friction between the media and the star, Lorrie always had the same relationship with her fans. Unfortunately, stardom was now beginning to change that too!

The fans, who used to be her best friends, had now, like the press, begun to crowd her and even scare her. Some were just too zealous and wanted to be too close. Some stalked her and her children. Others wrote threats. Morgan, 14, and Jesse, 8, were actually becoming frightened of the strange people who had been walking up to their door unannounced. Because of her concerns that some of the stranger ones might even act upon some deeply repressed fantasy and hurt her or her children, Lorrie purchased a more secure home. In a very real sense, her fame had now begun to cut her off from the real world she so deeply treasured. It was a sad day, one which her father never had to endure, when she was forced to put up that wall. It was almost like getting a divorce from her fans.

As Lorrie's sex symbol status grew, thanks in part to her sultry album covers, the swimsuit calendar, and her live show costuming, as she began to take on the aura of a country music superstar, her life became almost claustrophobic. She simply couldn't go out in public like she once had. She couldn't meet people as easily. She was always looking over her shoulder wondering if everything that she was doing was catching the eye of a crazed fan or a tabloid photographer. Sadly, when the media makes your records take a back seat to your personal life, as Reba, Barbara, Garth, and so many others had learned, your existence was then pretty much made up of working and hiding. This was the address where Lorrie now lived. The best moments of her life were in "the hiding place."

When Morgan did go out, it was more often than not to attend private parties or gatherings with other celebrities. These gatherings were safe and they offered a chance to visit with folks who had many things in common with Lorrie.

It was at one of these invitation-only gatherings, an industry fundraiser for a Republican senatorial candidate, where Lorrie met Fred Thompson. The fifty-two-year-old former actor hardly seemed Morgan's type. He was balding, mixed up in the world of politics, the father of three grown children, and a man whose time was hardly his own. He certainly wasn't Troy Aikman. Yet within weeks of that first meeting, Thompson was taking Morgan on his arm at major political events as well as showing up to watch her work the Opry. The soon-to-be senator was completely smitten.

Lorrie seemed drawn to Thompson too. Much of this attraction may have come from the fact that he could speak so intelligently about so many different subjects. She had never known anyone quite like him. He wasn't focused on just one area of life, he was a part of scores of things. In spite of his conservative politics and appearance, he was exciting in ways that Troy or Keith had never been. Thompson was well-educated. He was an attorney who had worked as an actor in seventeen major films. Some of these, such as *In the Line of Fire, No Way Out, The Hunt for Red October*, and *Cape Fear*, had been heralded as the best films of the era. He was confident, bold, and well-known. He also understood the demands of Lorrie's business. Yet even as they flew from coast to coast to see each other, even as the couple snuggled like teenagers in dark corners at parties, few gave the new romance much of a chance at lasting more than a few months. Most figured that their careers would pull them apart before they could ever come completely together.

While Lorrie had spent much of 1993 simply holding her own professionally, her career caught between climbing up and falling down, the publicity she had managed to garner from her two very public romances with a jock and a politician had boosted Morgan's profile a great deal in 1994. She had hit a place reserved for some very special people, such as Demi Moore or Sharon Stone. It didn't matter if her releases weren't hitting the top, she had achieved an image that seemed to indicate that she was always at the top anyway.

Lorrie's emergence into the national big time was probably best signaled by being chosen to host the ABC television network's *American Music Awards*. Newspapers around the country trumpeted the news that Morgan would join Queen Latifah and Tom Jones at the Shrine Auditorium in Los Angeles on January 30, to preside over one of the nation's fastest growing awards shows. This wasn't like hosting the ACMs where only country was displayed, this was the world's music, and only stars that were recognized by the whole world could anchor this show. For Lorrie, who wasn't scoring at the CMA awards show, this was fitting revenge.

Even though Nashville's music establishment now largely ignored her, instead handing out awards and nominations to the likes of Mary Chapin Carpenter and newcomer Shania Twain, neither of whom had Music City roots, Lorrie would not turn her back on the city and industry she loved so dearly. Even though she probably would have been welcomed with open arms in Los Angeles, no one had to worry about Lorrie Morgan deserting Nashville for Hollywood. She was staying put.

One of country's most astute voices, Robert K. Oerman, wrote in the March, 1995 *Washington Post* that Lorrie was a "throwback." And he was probably right. In an era where the Shania Twains of the world were created in studios via catchy tunes and videos, Lorrie was from the hard-working, rung-by-rung, up-the-ladder school of success. She was out-front and public. And as much as her fame allowed her, she was accessible to her fans and the media. There was no mystery, just honesty.

And if you thought she was good in the studio, she was even better in person. She had earned her status, unlike some others—it had not been given to her.

Compared to the hoopla involved in Twain's almost manufactured emergence, Lorrie had almost quietly recorded three albums that had sold more than a million copies a piece. She had also had numerous hit singles that out-climbed other more awarded stars, including Carpenter. She had made her record company more than $25 million. How many women could claim that? And after doing all of this, she had still refused to turn her back on the place where she started, the Opry. The fans loved her! So why wasn't this beautiful woman even more popular with the establishment? Why was it that Music City seemed to want to keep her from winning the awards she would have seemed to have deserved?

In truth it was probably the assertive quality of the woman herself that was beginning to alienate Lorrie from a great number of her past Music City fans within the industry. They liked her better as a shy little girl looking for a break than they did a confident star tossing around her weight. Even in the nineties, a woman with a take-charge attitude did not go over well in the male-controlled world of country music.

"A lot of people don't like that about me," she told Oerman when he interviewed her backstage at the Opry. "I will stand up for what I believe in." And she continued to do that more forcefully in and out of the studio.

In January, 1995, Lorrie made the news everywhere by landing on the arm of Senator Fred Thompson at the Tennessee gubernatorial inaugural ball. While she wouldn't answer any questions about their relationship, she did seem to resemble Cinderella with her Prince. There was a glow about the young woman that had been absent since Troy Aikman had left her. Fred was glowing too!

As time went on, Lorrie discovered that she felt more comfortable with Thompson than any man she had dated since Keith Whitley's death. The spotlight didn't bother him, he already had a family, so he had no desire for the children she couldn't give, and he liked her music without being jealous of the attention she received everywhere she went. Though he was not as young or as good-looking as most of the men who had come and gone in Lorrie's parade of romances, he certainly had the charm and intelligence to rival any of them. Maybe for the first time in Morgan's life, this pairing was more a relationship about comfort and communication than passion. Yet it was also about growth.

Thompson had renewed Lorrie's interest in acting. With Fred's encouragement, she again began to seek out parts. She even managed to land a small supporting role in the ABC telemovie *The Enemy Within*. The movie stared Gerald McRaney. Lorrie played Barbara Holloran, a friend of McRaney's on-screen wife. Yet even though the experience had to have been better than *Proudheart*, Lorrie had her reservations about wanting to really throw herself into acting on a regular basis. The weeks on the set had again been confining. She informed *TV Guide* that acting was simply "too demanding." It was also a field where Morgan wasn't allowed to be assertive.

Too big to travel alone, Lorrie was now almost always a part of a package road show booked into huge arenas. She no longer sang for hundreds, she sang for tens of thousands. In her little spare time, the hours when she wasn't touring, acting or spending time with her senator, Morgan was working with such stars as Alan Jackson, Tracy Lawrence, Joe Diffe, and Ricky Skaggs on a Keith Whitley tribute album. Yet just as it had when Aikman had been calling her signals, most everything in her life now seemed to be taking a back seat to her latest romance.

The March 27, 1995 issue of *USA Today* trumpeted the hot relationship between Lorrie and Fred Thompson was growing hotter. The Tennessee Republican admitted that the couple was a couple at the 110th Gridiron Club dinner. He announced his position right there in front of most of the major players in U.S. politics, including the President of the United States, Bill Clinton. Thompson would tell Dick Zimmerman, "She's a very special person in my life."

Thompson probably felt more and more drawn to Morgan because Lorrie had come to grips with who she was. She was thirty-five and the singer really seemed to be comfortable with herself. She wasn't worried about being called a bitch, she was no longer living in the shadow of Keith Whitley's tragic death, and she wasn't having to work hard just to get someone to notice her. Much more than a star, she was a woman who had the confidence to be who she wanted to be.

Lorrie was vampish, yet she retained a bit of the all-American cheerleader quality that seemed to diffuse any threat she might offer to women. This look and attitude didn't seemed to be calculated, she simply was both sexy and the girl-next-door at the same time. She was also a hard-nosed businesswoman and a sweet and kind mother. She was a fighter and a lover. She was demanding, and yet she was giving. And she loved to try new things, but she would never sacrifice tradition to make a career move. She was obviously a woman who embraced a deep faith, yet she also peppered her interviews with mild profanity. She knew the importance of fans, but also sought her privacy now more than ever. Almost every self-assured man was drawn to her too! Yet Fred had gotten there first.

Even though she knew and liked the person and entertainer Lorrie Morgan, even though she could walk away from the business knowing she had accomplished more than anyone would have dreamed possible for George's little girl, just knowing these facts did not completely satisfy Lorrie. Even with her plate full, she was still hungry. The little woman with the big dreams felt she had much to accomplish and the clock was ticking. She knew that in the career of a country music star, there were no time outs.

In spite of what she had told *TV Guide* just a few months before, one of her goals since coupling with Thompson was to make some kind of impact as an actress. Yet she had to do it on her own terms. Neither of her first acting experiences had allowed her much input. On those jobs, Lorrie had felt stifled. When CBS brought her an idea that showed some merit, it convinced Lorrie that just maybe she could act under her own terms. CBS's concept was the pilot for a series called *Loralie Lee*. The sitcom's script had been written with Lorrie in mind.

At first *Loralie Lee* seemed made to order for the singer. The concept centered on country music, the show was to be filmed in Nashville, and Lorrie would be given room to expand and grow as an actress. Then, when the actual pilot was filmed, the show made a dramatic change. The CBS crew who took charge of production didn't seem to have a clue as to what country music really was. Their ideas were not to show the new Nashville, but to create a Nashville that was filled with bales of hay, cornpone humor, and big hair. *Loralie Lee* had turned into *Hee Haw* meets *Mary Tyler Moore*. Lorrie lived up to the obligations of her contract, but had little or no control over the final product. The singer was probably grateful that the series was never picked up. Not having this project thrust upon the American public might just have saved her a great deal of embarrassment with her peers and fans.

Even if the final product has been high quality, it was fortunate that *Loralie Lee* didn't work out. A weekly television show would have placed even more strain on Morgan's already stretched life. Ultimately it was something that she really didn't need at this time. A series, coupled with her music and her family, wouldn't have given Lorrie much time to even think of doing other things. And that would have been very sad, because even though CBS didn't want her, other entertainment giants did.

Frank Sinatra called and asked Lorrie to do a duet with him to celebrate his eightieth birthday. Lorrie did so well with her first cut on *Frank Sinatra Duets II,* that they cut another. And her songs, "How Do You Keep" and "Funny Valentine," were picked by many critics as the best on the highly publicized CD. Other artists who joined the Chairman of the Board included Stevie Wonder, Gladys Knight, Linda Ronstadt, Willie Nelson, Lena Horne, Neil Diamond, Patti LaBelle, Jimmy Buffett, Steve Lawrence, and Eydie Gorme. Yet it would be Lorrie who stole the show and Frank's heart. And Sinatra wasn't the only expert she impressed as she made the concert rounds during the year.

In a July 17 review, the *Boston Herald*'s Sarah Rodman trumpeted Ms. Morgan's style and ability to relate to her fans. From top to bottom, the writer seemed to appreciate the concert, pointing out how at ease this country music superstar was onstage. She closed the offering by writing, "Ending the evening with her lovely, and campy, ballad 'Something in Red,' Morgan successfully wed her two styles. The weepy pedal steel to the pop melody, the tear-in-my-beer lyric with the synthesized strings showed why Morgan, and the best of the new country artists, have found such a wide audience."

When not on the road, Lorrie was most often seen on a new senator's arm, but she usually refused to speak of their relationship to the press. "It is private and I want to keep it that way," she explained to reporters. The close-mouthed response was probably the result of having had so much made of her past quotes concerning relationships with other beaus, especially Troy Aikman. Lorrie had learned the hard way that the tabloids were going to hang on her every remark and then twist it to make a story. She was simply tired of feeding them. If the rags were going to write about her, then they were going to have to go to someone other than her for the story. As she would find out, they would.

Yet the tabloid press didn't drag Lorrie through the fire all the time. They occasionally gave her some good ink! Because she was country music's most obvious bombshell a throw back to the glamour and sex appeal of a Marilyn Monroe, she often found the clothes she wore highlighted in color spreads at the newsstand. The *Star* even went so far as to call Ms. Morgan "Nashville's Most Sophisticated Lady," and give her a full-page color spread that showed the lady off in five different outfits. The publication loved the fact that Lorrie took chances, but took those risks with class and style. Her outfits might have been hot, but they were always in the best of taste. They showed off her outstanding figure without revealing too much of her hidden assets. In an issue that went to great lengths to make fun of the likes of most of country music's other female stars, Lorrie came out on top! Yet at about that same time she was ruling the fashion parade, the singer's health was again bottoming out.

In August, Lorrie's jetsetter pace finally caught up with her. She was forced to cancel part of a tour due to exhaustion, chest congestion, and a severe cough. Doctors ordered her to take it easy for three weeks. During this time of ordered rest Lorrie finally and formally admitted to *New Country* that it was time for her to move on past Keith Whitley. She loved him and always would, but he was in the past and she had to keep that part of her life in perspective. She told the magazine that she simply could no longer live her life and try to live his as well. He would have to live on through his music and people's memories, but not as a part of every moment of her day.

In September, a now-rested Lorrie finally let down her guard about the new man in her life. She informed *TV Guide* that Thompson was "the only man I've ever met who understands me. And the happier I am, the better I write. I wrote the best song I have ever written last night. It's called 'One Down and One More to Go.'" As she would soon find out, the senator who was inspiring her creativity would soon be the next one to go!

Her music, almost forgotten because of her well-publicized romances, jumped back into the spotlight when BNA released the single "Back in Your Arms Again" in late summer. The single was good, it got solid airplay, but it didn't create the rush that some of Morgan's earlier releases had. Yet the numbers were still good enough to keep her following the path she and her father had once dreamed that Lorrie would take.

In a very real sense, Lorrie got the opportunity to really follow in her father's footsteps when she launched a new concert series with the Nashville Symphony in November. George had been the first Opry performer to sing with a symphony, and now the torch was being picked up by another generation. Joining with Principle Pops conductor Ron Huff, like her father, Lorrie was going to sing with the best of Music City's elite musicians. Huff, who had arranged works for Amy Grant, Clint Black, and Donna Summer, called the opportunity to hear Morgan with the symphony a "rare treat." The show also provided a very public forum for Lorrie to again trumpet a special note about her private life. She dedicated "Faithfully" to a local senator during both of her shows.

Some country music performers would have given almost anything to have added two dates with the Nashville Symphony to their bio. This would have been the biggest news of the years for scores of acts. Yet for Lorrie it was just a warm-up. And just the announcement of the revolutionary real show would bring in media from all parts of the country.

In the late fall, the Kraft Country Tour announced that they would sponsor a country music showcase that featured singers Lorrie Morgan, Pam Tillis, and Carlene Carter as headliners in 1996. The 33-city tour, which would last from the last week of May 1996 to September 1996, thus became the first country music tour to be headlined by only women. Booking arrangements were coordinated by two giants, William Morris Agency and Buddy Lee Attractions. The tour was even planning video segments showing the family heritage of each act. A part of the proceeds would benefit the Second Harvest Food Bank and be used to feed homeless and hungry people all across the nation. In other words, this was a big deal, so big a deal that the announcement even ran on the AP wire and in *USA Today*.

Marty Stuart had long called the three women the "Opry Brats." This was a direct play on the ladies having grown up backstage while their parents worked the audience. Yet the fact that the trio was a part of country music history was not lost on Kraft. After all, Kraft had been sponsoring country music on television since the time when most video images were black and white. Because of this knowledge of the genre and its fans, Kraft didn't anticipate any trouble selling tickets for the all-female event. Robert Hopton, director of marketing for Kraft, confidently stated, "We were looking forward to doing something that hadn't been done before and also looking for heritage in country music. With the talent of these women on this stage, how could we go wrong?"

"It is unique and something that I've been wanting to do for awhile," Tony Conway of Buddy Lee Attractions chimed in. "It's also something the girls have been wanting to do."

At the press conference Ms. Morgan added, "It is a wonderful day when three women in country music can pull off a tour."

Meanwhile Pam, who had probably given the movers and shakers the idea in the first place simply sounded humble. "I feel Kraft is giving us the opportunity to make some wonderful memories on this tour." And a lot of money too!

"The Opry Brats" were scheduled to journey to places such as Birmingham, Alabama; Charlotte and Raleigh, N.C.; Chicago; Cleveland and Columbus, Ohio; Denver, Colorado; Detroit and Grand Rapids, Michigan; Evansville, Indiana; Dallas, Houston, and San Antonio, Texas; Indianapolis, Indiana; St. Louis and Kansas City, Missouri; Memphis, Nashville, and Knoxville, Tennessee; Little Rock, Arkansas; Los Angeles, California; Louisville, Kentucky; Milwaukee, Wisconsin; Minneapolis, Minnesota; Syracuse/Buffalo and New York City, New York; Oklahoma City, Oklahoma; Omaha/Lincoln, Nebraska; Phoenix, Arizona; Richmond, Virginia; Tampa, Florida; and Washington, D.C. They had been guaranteed the finest production that money could buy. They were assured that while it was their show to work, the sky was still the limit. They could do what they wanted as long as the fans approved. With long lines of men and women lining up for tickets, there was no doubt that this event would start a trend. Lorrie was extremely happy to be at the front of this revolutionary charge.

Country music songwriters have long dwelled on the truth in Murphy's Law. The scribes seemed to always know that when everything was going perfectly, that it simply meant that things were about to fall apart. Lorrie probably couldn't have guessed it then, but the new year offered a hint that the songwriters and Murphy knew a great deal about Morgan's love life. Yet for now, everything was coming up roses!

Chapter 15

Richard McVey II wrote about Lorrie Morgan in *Music City News,* "When she sings of heartbreak, it's because she lived it. If she vocalizes losses in her life, she can back it up. She has weathered the hard times, thrived during the good, and grew up somewhere in between."

And certainly Lorrie was all grown up. And in the first few days of 1996, she was heavily involved in promoting new product. The first project that she wanted to talk about was one that she had decided was needed to fully inform the industry and the public just how much they had lost when her second husband had died.

Even though he had been dead for seven years, and even though his ghost no longer haunted her, Lorrie had refused to let go of his genius. With the input of some of Whitley's best friends and Nashville's greatest talents, Lorrie had helped put together a tribute album. *Wherever You Are Tonight* featured ten new Whitley tunes highlighting the singer's crooning style (another seventeen were unreleased and in the RCA vaults). As the sales figures came in, Lorrie discovered that the fans had not forgotten the man whose voice Ms. Morgan called the "greatest to ever sing country music." Yet Keith's body of work was not the only body that Lorrie was promoting.

Morgan used the pages of *Country Weekly* to promote her second annual pin-up calendar. This one featured the singer in sexy lingerie. At first glance, many readers may have thought they had picked up a Victoria's Secret catalog, rather than a country music trade publication. After taking a second look, and most people did, they discovered that this was a periodical dedicated to promoting entertainment not sleepwear.

In an interview that accompanied the pictorial, Lorrie told the magazine that the softly lit photos really did reflect a side of her that few people knew. "I think there is some truth to me being tough, but I also think I'm soft and sentimental—sometimes too soft for my own good."

The woman who had gained the reputation as one of Nashville's toughest ladies, admitted to *Country Weekly* that she cried at movies and weddings. Yet when asked if she would soon be crying at her own nuptials, she went back to talking about the pictures. For some reason the singer had gotten close-mouthed about Senator Fred Thompson again.

Obviously proud of the photo layout, Lorrie didn't feel that the calendar, which was long on leg and cleavage, was really very revealing. She called it "sensual." And while there was a lot of satin and silk, Morgan didn't ever strip down to her underwear for any of the shots. Like she always had before, she managed to keep her all-American image intact, though these pictures must have also showed *Playboy* just how much they were missing by not being able to interest the star into displaying her charms in their pages.

In matters closer to the heart, the rumors of a Lorrie Morgan/Fred Thompson split-up began to make the rounds in March, but it was late May before the duo's parting became official. Even then, Lorrie was less than specific about the facts concerning the passing of one of Washington's most talked about romances. She wouldn't say it was over, even when some of her "friends" had leaked the word to the tabloids.

"I'm not sure that it is a romance right now," she finally admitted. Then she added, "I'd rather not talk about it. . . . You know what? The thing is, I'm not looking. For the first time in my life, I'm not looking."

To many in Music City, it might have seemed like big news that Lorrie wasn't on the prowl, yet in all honesty this might have just been a part of the growth that those close to her had noted. Lorrie was now really strong enough to stand on her own. She was happy within her own life. Anything more than this happiness and contentment was simply a bonus.

"I love men," a wiser Lorrie explained. "I love romance. But I can't make that happen. It's time to wait for it to find you. I'm happy with my children, my life, my career. I'm free and can come and go as I please; I don't have to answer to anybody."

Lorrie told Phyllis George on TNN's *Spotlight With Phyllis* that she and Senator Fred Thompson had talked about marriage, but before that she had wanted to marry Troy Aikman, "probably more than I've ever wanted anything in my life." Lorrie blamed tabloid newspapers for the demise of the relationship with the quarterback. During the interview she observed, "You hear something in Dallas or you hear something in Nashville, and you're not there to look at each other eye to eye. You can call each other on the phone and you hear it, and right away you accuse the other one. And it tore our relationship up. It totally destroyed us."

In a sense that might have been what tore Fred and Lorrie apart too. They just didn't have enough one-on-one time together. And as soon as Thompson had disappeared, Lorrie's friends sensed that the singer missed Thompson's intellect and knowledge. Most of those around her seemed to believe that while she would fall in love again, after meaningful and fulfilling flings with a football player and a senator, it was going to take someone really special to turn her head now.

Lorrie herself admitted that now she simply couldn't be involved with a normal man. Because she had seen so much, done so much, and been so many places, she needed someone who had experienced a great deal of life beyond a normal existence too. In a very real sense she admitted that she didn't want to teach someone, she wanted to learn from them. That learning experience was probably the most important thing she had taken from her time with Thompson, and she wouldn't be satisfied without it now. As she told *Howdy* magazine, "It becomes a place where you need someone who knows what the hell is goin' on . . .'' Most women didn't see a whole lot of those types around either.

Yet even though she was now comfortable with her life and herself, and even though she wasn't interested in seriously dating at this time, Lorrie simply didn't like to be alone. Usually she took one of her sisters with her on the road. She needed this company just to help sort out emotions and ideas. She also knew that when you were with someone you loved, you were stronger than when you were all by yourself.

Because she had been a part of the country music scene since she was very small, Lorrie had watched others try to make it on their own. She had seen stars firsthand deal with the bad days on the road without a close friend to lean on. And when the times were tough, and when there was no one there to whom to talk, many of these performers turned to alcohol, drugs, and sex. Morgan was not about to let herself go down that same road. So to be strong, she admitted her weaknesses and made sure that she had help beside her whenever she needed it.

In April BNA announced the Lorrie's *Greatest Hits* album had gone platinum. This mark was passed less than eight months after the record's release. Riding on the crest of this success, the label announced that Lorrie's new album, *Greater Need*, would be in stores in June.

June 9, 1996 was the date that the follow up to *War Paint* was officially released. This was Lorrie's first completely new album in more than a year. A great deal was expected of it too. This LP needed to duplicate the success of Lorrie's first two albums, not the last one.

Greater Need's first single, ''I Didn't Know My Own Strength,'' had been her theme song in concerts for some time. The song was almost autobiographical and was one of Morgan's personal favorites. In the lyrics a great deal of what Lorrie had had to find out about herself as tragedies have hit her life was revealed note by note and bar by bar. And perhaps because of the emotion revealed in both the video and the single, fans and country radio bought into this song in a very big way. ''I Didn't Know

My Own Strength'' would become Lorrie's best record in two years.

People magazine was one of the many magazines sold on Lorrie's *Greater Need*. In their review, the periodical pointed out that while Reba may have won the lion's share of the awards, Lorrie sold product just as well. The magazine's Randy Vest noted, ''Her mantel may not be filling up with statuettes, but *Greater Need* keeps Morgan planted firmly in the big leagues.'' A few weeks later her mantel did get a new keepsake as Lorrie won a trophy at the TNN/Music City News awards for Female Vocalist of the Year. Adding a bit of spice to this victory was the fact that Reba had struck out. So the ''mantel'' itself might have been seemed to be passing from the redhead to the blonde.

Yet the mere fact that Reba was finally sliding a bit while Lorrie was now rising again was not enough to push Morgan directly to the top of country music. The emergence of Shania Twain had not eclipsed the success Lorrie had enjoyed over the past six years, but Shania's meteoric rise had left many wondering what was wrong with country music and this ever-changing star system. It also gave BNA cause to worry.

Few would argue that Twain was a manufactured star. Attractive, blessed with a sexy body, and a seemingly solid voice, she had never paid her dues. As a matter of fact, the Canadian hadn't even toured. She had indicated that she wouldn't tour until she released at least two albums! Her hits had been generated in the studio, as had her personality up until this point. No one really knew who she was or what to think of her talent. The only time she mixed with the public was during autograph sessions and awards. And even on these opportunities, she rarely sang live. In other words, she had become a superstar while breaking every one of the old rules about how to become a country music star, as well as how to stay one.

For someone like Lorrie, who had spent more than half of her life doing it the right way, this type of quick and undeserving success must have seemed grossly unfair. Yet if she felt that way, no one knew it. While others cried foul, Morgan welcomed Twain to the business and then went on about hers as if nothing had changed. Lorrie was able to handle Shania's quick rise so well because the older singer had seen it happen before. She was a veteran.

Lorrie recognized, much more than others, that you could be hot one moment and cold the next. She knew that success was temporal at best. After all the highs came the lows. In country music even the best came crashing down. And usually the quicker you got to the top, the quicker you became a has been. Twain's fame would end, and for that matter, at some time, so would Lorrie's. When that happened you had to look at the real person who you had become on the trip to the top, not the former star who used to be somebody. And if you hadn't become somebody who you could feel comfortable with—someone of real substance—then you were going to have real problems when the world stopped crying out your name.

One of the ways Lorrie prepared for this day was by keeping folks around her who were honest and straightforward. If they didn't like something, they told her. If they thought she screwed up, they informed her.

Lorrie would often say that being the true friend of a star was tough. Morgan had seen many superstars who had grown so important that everyone laughed at every one of their jokes, funny or not, and catered to every one of their whims, wise or not. While Lorrie took the bows, the folks who were perceived as background players and had no worth in the eyes of most media and fans kept the singer on track to be a part of the real world. For that reason, and many a host of others that most big stars wouldn't recognize, these humble people were treated with great respect by the star. She knew that while her true friends cared nothing about the fame or glory, they cared a great deal about her. They would be there when the party was over. She only hoped that folks like Shania had the same kind of good people around her too.

The need for honesty was probably why Lorrie had long felt so comfortable at the Opry. These people cared about each other. They were a family. In a very real sense they were all on common ground. Those who really loved Morgan shuddered to even consider how the singer would have gotten through her life without that Opry family. They had been there every time she had needed them.

Lorrie had shared why she loved the Opry so much with Robert K. Oermann in 1995: "I can't get next to half of the female artists who are out there right now. It's all so competitive. These people here at the Opry don't care about that. All the ladies here are my buddies. It's like, 'We're friends in country music. Let's hang out.' The Opry is about sharing."

And sharing was so important to Lorrie now. She was the mother of a teenager and having to deal with dates. She had a son who played ball. She had a mother who liked to spoil her grandkids. And she had the Opry to share with all of them.

So, up or down, Lorrie remained a dreamer with her feet firmly planted on solid ground. As she told *USA Today* in 1995, "I still am a firm believer in fairy tales. I feel that I'm very fortunate that with all the tragedy and hard things I've been through, I still believe in romance and I still believe in happily ever after." Yet in the singer's mind, happily ever after could only happen when combined with her music.

If she ever falls in love again, the first place she will probably bring her man is the Opry. It is on that simple stage that the pin-up model, the tragic heroine, the superstar, and the assertive business woman really gets to drop all the airs. It is on this stage, the one where her father charmed thousands each week with his "Candy Kisses," that Lorrie is really at home. And it is here where all of her real dreams have begun, and it will be here where they will probably all be fulfilled.

Lorrie told *Country Weekly* in early 1996, "My main love is country. That's where I was brought up, that's what I sing, that's what I want to sing ninety percent of the time. My deepest wish is to win Entertainer of the

Year and wind up in the Hall of Fame while I'm still alive.''

And if that ever happens, the awards and honor will be given to Lorrie at her home, the Grand Ole Opry. And somewhere offstage, just out of sight of the audience, right behind the edge of the curtain, the image of George Morgan will be there, smiling, crying, and cheering his little girl on.

THE TRUE STORY OF A NASHVILLE DAUGHTER'S RISE TO GLORY

Out of Her Father's Shadow

ACE COLLINS

Born to Nashville royalty, Mel Tillis's daughter Pam would pay a heavy price before claiming her crown as one of country music's most successful female vocalists. Read her inspiring story of tragedy over triumph— as she bravely rises above a near-fatal car crash and many other harrowing obstacles on her way to legendary country music fame.

PAM TILLIS
Ace Collins
0-312-96404-8___$5.99 U.S.___$7.99 Can.